FORT BRIDGER

FORT BRIDGER

Island in the Wilderness

Fred R. Gowans

Eugene E. Campbell

Brigham Young University Press

Cover: Washakie, Chief of the Shoshone, observed the changing scenes at Fort Bridger while guiding his people wisely for sixty years in their relations with mountain men, immigrants, Mormons, soldiers, and federal Indian agents, as well as with other Indian tribes.

Library of Congress Cataloging in Publication Data

Gowans, Fred R   1936-
    Fort Bridger, island in the wilderness.

    Based in part on F. R. Gowans' thesis.
    Includes bibliographical references.
    1. Fort Bridger, Wyo.—History. 2. Mormons and Mormonism in Wyoming. 3. Bridger, James, 1804-1881. I. Campbell, Eugene E., 1915- joint author. II. Title.
    F769.F54G68   978.7'85'020924   75-5827
    ISBN 0-8425-0419-2
    ISBN 0-8425-0420-6 pbk.

Library of Congress Number: 75-5827
International Standard Book Number: 0-8425-0419-2 (cloth)
                                     0-8425-0420-6 (paper)

Brigham Young University Press, Provo, Utah 84602
© 1975 Brigham Young University Press. All rights reserved
Printed in the United States of America
75 4700 p. 300 c   9964

Contents

Photographs

The Lewis Robison portrait on page 64 is reprinted by permission of the LDS Church Historical Department. Photographs on pages 13, 121, 144, 150, 153, 157, 158, 160 and 168 are printed by permission of author Fred R. Gowans. All other photographs are reprinted by permission of the Utah State Historical Society, Salt Lake City.

Documents

The following documents are reproductions of originals kept in the Church Archives, LDS Church Historical Department, Salt Lake City.

1. Letter dictated by Jim Bridger to Brigham Young, p. 39.
2. Shaver's warrant to Bridger, p. 51.
3. Ledger of goods used by the posse at Fort Bridger, p. 57.
4. Vasquez and Bridger receipt for $1,000, p. 58.
5. Robison's letter to Daniel H. Wells, p. 67.
6. Contract taken by Robison to Fort Bridger, p. 69.
7. Fort purchase contract, p. 72.
8. Contract verification of 1855, p. 73.
9. Letter from Lewis Robison verifying $4,000, p. 75.
10. Payment of gold-value difference, p. 75.
11. Inventory of merchandise, 1855, p. 177.

Maps

1. Various sites of Fort Bridger, p. 2.
2. Immigrant trails, pp. 16, 17.
3. State of Deseret and territory of Utah, p. 42.
4. Green River ferry sites, p. 45.
5. Dimensions of cobblestone wall, p. 80.
6. Dimensions of cobblestone wall with alternate position of corral, p. 81.
7. Routes followed by U.S. Army expedition in 1857-58, pp. 96, 97.
8. Dimensions of military Fort Bridger with lunettes, p. 107.
9. Military fort with alternate position of corral, p. 107.
10. Location of Camp Floyd, p. 110.
11. General location of Indian tribes, p. 139.
12. Union Pacific Railroad route, p. 154.
13. Present highways in the Fort Bridger area, p. 164.

Foreword

In human history, trade has ever been a prominent feature of life. Centers for barter developed at the crossings of travel routes, growing in size and importance as the traffic increased. Crossroads on land were important, but transfer of goods from water to land and vice versa were generally more significant in promoting and enlarging centers of trade.

Earliest and easiest travel in the American West was on rivers. So water transportation was utilized and early trading posts were established on the Missouri River and its navigable branches. But as fur men penetrated the central Rockies they came into territory without navigable rivers. In such a region Fort Bridger was to come into existence. For this outpost and similar ones horses and mules were the only means of transport.

The first trade in this western country was carried on between white men and Indians. Later, as whites took up fur-trapping, much of the trade was conducted between trappers and their business-wise suppliers of equipment and goods.

The annual *Rendezvous*, a temporary and movable trade fair, was introduced in 1825. It was cheaper than maintaining a permanent trading post, and it served trade requirements well. The factors that determined a good site were an open valley, ample water, and abundant grass for the horses that provided transportation for men and goods.

The *rendezvous* was short-lived. As furs diminished they were supplanted by buffalo robes, and the *rendezvous* gave way to the trading post, or fort. Then as fur animals, buffalo, and other game were killed off, the Indians' food supply and trade items diminished, and their economy and very lives were threatened.

An important new development that increased the Indians' difficulties was the coming of land-hungry emigrants seeking homes in the West. Lengthening trains of covered wagons rutted the pack horse trails and frightened away the game. As the wagons emptied their loads of settlers upon the choicest lands, the Indians grew restive. Accompanying or following the emigrants came dragoons and foot soldiers to protect the travel routes of the white men. The government took over many of the early trading posts and converted them into military forts. The new conditions changed the relations between the two races from peaceful trade to constant conflict.

As hostilities continued between the grasping white settlers and the protesting Indians, the first military forts were reinforced and numerous new ones were established. Vigorous campaigns against the red men were launched as increasing and expanding settlements demanded the expulsion or elimination of the Indians.

The wars of the 1870s and 1880s with the Indians were finally terminated by the disreputable confrontation at Wounded Knee in 1890. The same year marked the abandonment of Fort Bridger and Fort Laramie. Dozens of other forts were dismantled before or after these two. A period of American history punctuated by many bloody events came to an end.

It is interesting to observe how quickly some of the significant and romantic acts of the Western drama passed across the stage of history. The fur traders' *rendezvous* lasted but sixteen years (1825-40); the burro and mule trains of the Old Spanish Trail moved between Santa Fe and Los Angeles but eighteen years (1830-48); the overland stagecoach careened to the Pacific for only twenty years (1849-69); the open range cattle herds followed the long trail northward for twenty years (about 1865-85); and the main Indian Wars of the West reddened the plains for about three decades (the 1860s to 1880s).

Fur trade posts dotted the map of the West during most of the early nineteenth century. Lewis and Clark established Fort Mandan on the upper Missouri in 1804; Manuel Lisa founded Fort Manuel at the mouth of the Bighorn in 1811; Astor's men built Fort Astor on the Columbia in 1811. The fur trade of the West burgeoned in the 1830s. Forts Laramie, Hall, and Boise were built in 1834. Hiram M. Chittenden, the first great historian of the American fur trade, located scores of fur trade posts on his excellent map; many of these were converted into military forts.

Fort Bridger was the first emigrant way station, the initial trading post established specifically to serve the covered wagon trains to the far West. It was a notable trading outpost. Not only did it supply westbound emigrants, but it catered also to the Indian trade. It played an important part in the so-called "Mormon War" of 1857-58 and then became a United States military fort and continued that role until 1890, the year generally accepted as the termination

viii

of the Frontier. During almost a half century it was a notable outpost of the American West.

A number of other Western forts have already inspired book-length narratives. It is gratifying that at long last we now have a worthy account of historic Fort Bridger.

LeRoy R. Hafen
Professor Emeritus of History
Brigham Young University

Trappers and Indians meet to exchange goods, from a painting by A. J. Miller.

Introduction

Fort Bridger, founded in the declining days of the fur trade, was the first post built in the West for emigrant trade. Its importance in western American history is hardly subject to question. Hiram Chittenden, famous authority on the American Fur Trade, considered it to be the second most important post on the Oregon Trail. The fort played a prominent role in the final years of the fur trade, the history of the Shoshone and Bannock Indians, the Oregon Trail, the development of the Hastings' cutoff, Mormon emigration, the gold rush, overland transportation, freighting and communications, plus its own military history before 1890 when it was abandoned. During early years the fort had three different owners: James Bridger and Louis Vasquez (1842-55), the Mormon Church (1855-57), and the Federal Government (1857-90). It is now owned by the state of Wyoming.

This study presents a detailed history of each of these periods. The account covering the first two periods is based on the Ph.D. dissertation of Dr. Fred R. Gowans, with information drawn from journals, records of the Church of Jesus Christ of Latter-day Saints, government documents, and other primary sources. Some secondary sources such as C. G. Coutant, *History of Wyoming and The Far West* (3 vols.), Andrew Jenson's, "History of Fort Bridger and Fort Supply," *Utah Genealogical and Historical Magazine*, IV (1913), and Milton R. Hunter, *Brigham Young the Colonizer*, have been helpful.

New source materials for this study have come primarily from the Manuscript Collection, Journal History and private journals and diaries at the LDS

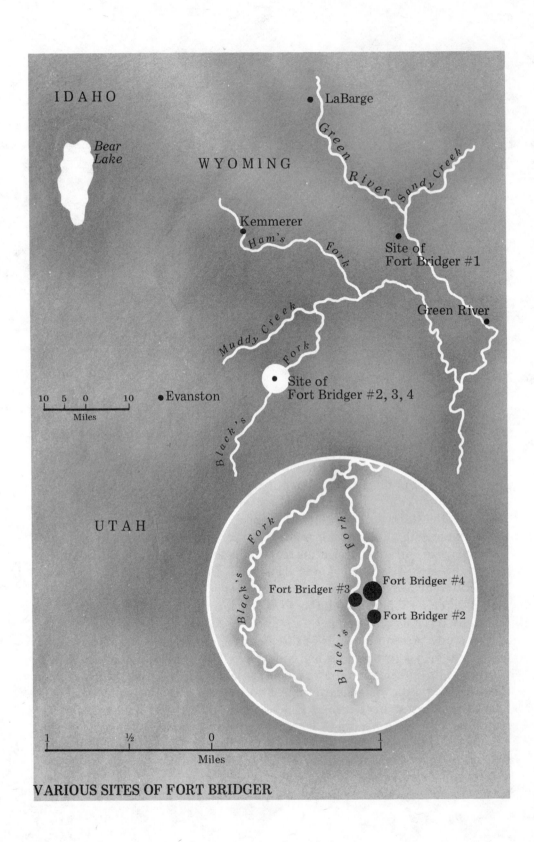

VARIOUS SITES OF FORT BRIDGER

Church Historical Department in Salt Lake City, Utah. The Manuscript Collections at the Utah and Wyoming State Historical Societies, and the manuscripts in the Special Collections at the University of Wyoming, University of Utah, and Brigham Young University, have also provided valuable information. The National Archives in Washington, D.C. supplied important film strips of the War Department and Commissioner of Indian Affairs' records.

In many direct quotations the authors have retained the original spelling and punctuation in order to preserve the flavor of the times, but for readability in some quotations they have made changes.

The authors have collaborated on this project in the following way. Dr. Gowans has done the primary research for the entire book and furnished a rough draft of the first six chapters. Dr. Campbell has rewritten the entire book, concentrating on organization and literary style. Working together has been a pleasant experience since the authors have so many interests in common including a common great grandfather who was an uncommon man.

The authors wish to acknowledge valuable services rendered by the following institutions and individuals in the production of this book: the Wyoming State Historical Society, the Utah State Historical Society, and the Historical Department of The Church of Jesus Christ of Latter-day Saints for helpfulness in providing documents and pictures; Dr. LeRoy R. Hafen, Professor of History, Emeritus, BYU, for his informative foreword; Marilyn M. Miller for her careful editing of the manuscript and enthusiastic support of the project; McRay Magleby for his supervision of the art work, and staff members Ron Eddington and Sydney Nethercott McDonald for their work on the cover and maps respectively.

1

James Bridger, famous mountain man, the colorful figure who founded the fort.

Jim Bridger settles down

James Bridger was one of approximately one hundred young men who answered the following notice which appeared in the *Missouri Republican* in St. Louis on 20 March 1822:

To Enterprising Young Men: The subscriber wishes to engage one hundred young men to ascend the Missouri River to its source, there to be employed for one, two, or three years. For particulars, inquire of Major Andrew Henry near the lead mines in the County of Washington, who will ascend with and command the party or the subscriber near St. Louis. — signed William H. Ashley.[1]

But approximately twenty years later, when Jim Bridger decided to settle down, he had become one of the most famous mountain men in the Rocky Mountain West and his name was destined to live on, associated with the fort that he helped to found. In the public mind, Jim Bridger, perhaps more than any other man in the fur trapping period, has become a symbol of the mountain men.

Young Jim was only three days from his nineteenth birthday when the advertisement appeared in the *Missouri Republican*. He had been born in Richmond, Virginia, on 17 March 1804, to James and Clarey Bridger, who were of Scottish descent. Jim's father, who kept a hotel in Richmond, and also had a large farm, moved his family to St. Louis in 1812. By 1817 the hardships of the frontier had left Jim the only surviving member of the family. He appren-

5

ticed to a local blacksmith and learned many skills which contributed to his success as a mountain man. By 1822, when the above item appeared in the paper, Jim Bridger felt qualified to apply and was anxious to live a life of adventure in the great trans-Mississippi West. During the next two decades he was to traverse almost every valley and mountain and cross every stream in the central part of the Rocky Mountains.

One of Bridger's first adventures brought him notoriety. He happened to be present at an unlucky encounter between mountain man Hugh Glass and a grizzly, which Jim Clyman described as follows:

Amongst the party was a Mr. Hugh Glass who could not be restrained . . . and kept under subordination. He went off the line of March one afternoon and met a large grizzly bear, . . . which he shot and wounded. . . . He attempted to climb a tree but the bear caught him and hauled him to the ground tearing and lacerating his body in fearful rate.[2]

Jim Bridger and another trapper, John Fitzgerald, volunteered—or were drafted—to remain with Hugh Glass and take care of him. Believing he could not live, however, they left him. Miraculously, Glass survived and found his way back to Fort Kiowa, some three hundred and fifty miles from the spot where he had been deserted. Some accounts of the incident state that Glass, although determined on revenge, excused Bridger because of his youth.

A year later, while trapping with Captain John H. Weber in northern Utah, Bridger decided to settle a wager as to the course of the Bear River, and descended it in a bull boat. He came upon a body of extremely salty water which he believed to be an arm of the Pacific Ocean, not realizing that he was on the shores of the Great Salt Lake. It is not certain that he was the first white man to see this important landmark, as there were other fur trappers and traders out of Taos in the region during that summer, but his visit is the first that is adequately documented. [3]

During the next decade Bridger worked for various fur companies. He attended Ashley's first rendezvous in 1825 on Henry's Fork and the second rendezvous in 1826 in Cache Valley. When Ashley sold his firm in 1826 to Jedediah Smith, David Jackson, and William Sublette, Bridger continued to work for them. In 1830 Sublette and his partners sold out to Bridger and his four partners, who adopted the name Rocky Mountain Fur Company. They spent the winter of 1830-31 deep in Blackfoot country on the Yellowstone River.

The new firm suffered a setback in 1831 when the supply caravan under Thomas Fitzpatrick did not arrive. By 1832 the company faced a formidable rival in the American Fur Company. Bridger and his partners, in search of pelts, decided to move into more dangerous Indian country, thus provoking skirmishes with the Indians. In one such skirmish, Bridger was shot in the back with an arrow which remained in his body until it was extracted by the Pres-

6

byterian missionary doctor Marcus Whitman, who happened to come to the rendezvous on the Green River in 1835. Describing this event, Samuel Parker wrote:

While we continued in this place, Dr. Whitman was called upon to perform some very important surgical operations. He extracted an iron arrow, three inches long from the back of Captain Bridger which was received in a skirmish three years before with the Blackfoot Indians. It was a difficult operation because the arrow was hooked at the point by striking a large bone and cartilaginous substance had grown around it. The doctor pursued the operation with great self possession and perseverance and the patient manifested equal firmness. [4]

Soon after this experience, Bridger married his first wife, Cora, who was the daughter of the Flathead chief, Insula.

The following year Bridger attended the rendezvous as usual—this one also located at the Green River site. Sometime later that year, in early fall or late summer, Bridger visited St. Louis and met a Scottish nobleman named William Drummond Stewart. Accompanying Stewart to the 1837 rendezvous was the famous artist Alfred J. Miller, who painted the scenes of the gathering for posterity. Actually Stewart had been in the West before and had gone back to Scotland, where he had inherited a title and considerable wealth. Now he had come West again to have one last fling in the mountains before returning to Scotland to fulfill his duties as a landed nobleman. Interestingly enough, Stewart brought Bridger a full suit of armor as a present, and the artist Miller sketched him on horseback in this unusual gift and placed him in his well-known painting "Rendezvous." Describing the painting, Miller wrote:

In the midst of them, Captain Bridger, in a full suit of steel armor, this gentleman was a famous Mountain Man and we venture to say that no one has traveled here within the last thirty years without seeing or hearing of him. The suit of armor was imported from England and presented to Captain B. by our commander. [5]

After the 1837 rendezvous, Bridger went north from the Green River as a pilot for Lucien B. Fontenelle and Company. The following year he left his family with his wife's tribe and went back to St. Louis. Here he met Father Pierre Jean de Smet, a Jesuit Priest, who became a close friend. Their paths crossed often in the western mountains.

Bridger returned to the rendezvous in the spring of 1839 by way of South Platte River where he visited with his old friend Louis Vasquez. On arriving at Green River the mountain men held their summer rendezvous, but by now many of Bridger's original companions had been killed or had retired. Only a few were present who had attended the colorful gatherings during the 1820s.

Louis Vasquez, Bridger's distinguished partner, was from an aristocratic family.

After the 1839 rendezvous, Bridger spent the fall around Henry's Fork of the Snake River. Winter found him again on the South Platte at Fort Vasquez. It was at this time that Bridger formed a partnership with Henry Fraeb and possibly with Louis Vasquez. In any case, these were the two men that Bridger began to talk with about the possibility of establishing trading posts, since it seemed apparent that the fur trapping and trading era was drawing to a close.

It is not certain where Bridger spent the latter part of 1840 or the first few months of 1841, but in July 1841, Jim Baker reported meeting him on Henry's Fork near Green River. In the summer of 1842 Colonel John C. Fremont, beginning his first exploration into the Rocky Mountain West, reported that he met Bridger and Vasquez leading a caravan en route to St. Louis. It was later that year that these two men left St. Louis to return to Black's Fork on the Green River and to build the trading post that became famous as Fort Bridger.

Louis Vasquez, Bridger's partner in this new enterprise, was not new to the West. Like Bridger, he was one of the young men who answered William Ashley's advertisement in the *Missouri Republican* and so began his western experience at the same time as Bridger. Born in 1798, he was a little older than Bridger and he was much better educated. Bernard DeVoto said that Louis Vasquez was of aristocratic birth like Fontenelle and that "bits of aristocratic elegance clung to him in the mountains like cottonwood fluff."[6] Colonel A. G. Brackett supported this image when he wrote in the palmy days of 1849 and

8

Looking southeast toward Bridger Valley, one can see the fort in the distance.

1850 that "Mr. Bridger and a partner named Vasquez, a Mexican who put on a great deal of style, used to ride around the country in a coach and four."[7]

Perhaps almost anyone would have seemed aristocratic compared to the rugged mountain man. Nevertheless, it was true Vasquez had come from a distinguished family and had received a reasonably good education. He began his career in the far west at the age of twenty-three, and evidence indicates he may have been in the region of the Great Salt Lake before Jim Bridger. Some credit him with having been the first white man to discover the lake. This has not been proven, but we do know he accompanied Robert Campbell and his caravan of supplies for the Rocky Mountain Fur Company to the rendezvous in 1833. On reaching Fort Laramie, he was given the task of locating the various groups of trappers and finding the exact location of the summer rendezvous. Even at this early date Robert Campbell recognized the talents of Vasquez, whose ability Jim Bridger capitalized on when he chose him for his partner at Fort Bridger. Vasquez had spent the winter of 1833-34 in the land of the Crow nation trading with members of the tribe. In the spring he brought his pelts to Fort William. His good friend of the Ashley days, Jim Beckworth, had been made a chief of the Crows and was living at that time with the tribe, which made it much easier for Vasquez to do business with them. At the end of the rendezvous of 1833, Vasquez was sent with all of the pelts acquired that season to the Big Horn River to construct boats and float the furs down the river to

9

St. Louis. For personal reasons, Vasquez stayed behind and traded with the Crow nation during that winter, losing all contact with his employers, and causing them to suspect he had lost his life. En route to the Green River, the supply train of 1834, led by William Sublette, found a note from Vasquez near Devil's Gate which brought a good deal of joy to the men who, having supposed that Vasquez was dead, now knew him to be alive.

Vasquez spent the winter of 1834-35 in the mountains around Vasquez Creek, a branch of the South Platte. It was here that he formed a partnership with Andrew Sublette that ultimately led to the building of Fort Vasquez in the fall of 1835 and the claim that he was the first white settler in the vicinity of Denver. In the summer of 1835 he was back in St. Louis handling affairs for his family. On July 29 of that year he and Sublette were issued a trading license by William Clark of Lewis and Clark fame, who then was superintendent of Indian affairs. Vasquez renewed this trading license in 1836, 1837, and 1838.

After Vasquez founded the fort on South Platte in 1839, it was reported that Jim Bridger visited there. It is doubtful that Vasquez was very happy with his business prospects at this time because of the vigorous competition with other nearby trading posts. Perhaps this rivalry led to their talk of establishing a trading post on the Green River to take advantage of the new emigration that was developing. Louis Vasquez and his partner, Andrew Sublette, sold their establishment in 1840, leaving Vasquez free to enter into a new relationship. Both he and Bridger were in St. Louis in the summer of 1842, and it is likely that this was the scene for the final arrangements between these two mountain men that resulted in the building of the famous Fort Bridger.

Interestingly enough, this was not the first Fort Bridger. Jim Bridger, in partnership with Henry Fraeb, had built a fort on the Green River between the mouths of the Big Sandy and Black's Fork in the midsummer of 1841. Evidently it was a substantial outpost because both Edwin Bryant and the Mormon William Clayton described it as having several log cabins. William Lorton, passing there in 1849, noted that cabins and chimneys were still standing and that a great quantity of cut wood gave evidence that someone had wintered there. It is not known how long Bridger occupied this fort, but his partner, Henry Fraeb, was killed by the Indians before the buildings were completed, which may be the reason the post was abandoned. Bridger moved into the Black's Fork region in the early summer of 1842 and constructed some buildings on the bluff overlooking Black's Fork, which became the second Fort Bridger. It was abandoned in less than a year, and in the spring of 1843 the third fort was started at the river bottoms and occupied by early August, 1843. This was the fort that became most famous and was later burned by the Mormons and rebuilt by the United States Army.

In view of the fact that both Jim Bridger and Louis Vasquez had been in the Rocky Mountain region for almost twenty years and had become acquainted with all of the major valleys, streams, and possible locations for trading posts, one wonders why they chose the particular spot they did. However, it should be recognized that the fort they built was the first post in the trans-Mississippi West constructed primarily for the purpose of engaging in the emigrant trade rather than the fur trade. This post then, was to mark an end to the fur-trading era. It was important, therefore, that it be located on the trail the emigrants were most likely to use. Black's Fork, a tributary of the Green River, provided a uniquely attractive location. Despite the fact that the region surrounding the area was a desolate wilderness, Black's Fork at this location divided into several smaller streams and formed a well-watered island in the wilderness. Grass grew in profusion, and willow trees provided shade. This was an excellent spot for travel-weary emigrants to stop and replenish their supplies. The post could support a large herd of horses which travelers could trade for the tired, jaded horses they had brought this far. So Bridger and Vasquez, knowing the region well, chose an excellent location for the post. On 10 December 1843 Bridger dictated a letter to Pierre Choteau and Company, hoping that firm would serve as his supplier of trading goods. In it he described the site of his fort:

I have established a small fort, with a blacksmith shop and a supply of iron in the road of the emigrants on Black's Fork of Green River, which promises fairly. In coming out they are generally well supplied with money, but by the time they get here they are in need of all kinds of supplies, horses provision, smithwork, etc. They bring ready cash from the states, and should I receive the goods ordered, will have considerable business in that way with them, and establish trade with the Indians in the neighborhood, who have a good number of beaver among them. The fort is a beautiful location on Black's Fork of Green River, receiving fine, fresh water from the snow on the Uintah range. The streams are alive with mountain trout. It passes the fort in several channels, each lined with trees, kept alive by the moisture of the soil. [8]

Edwin Bryant, who came west in 1846 accompanied by William H. Russell and eight other men on horseback, agreed with Jim Bridger's estimate of the location when he wrote of the fort:

Its position is in a handsome and fertile bottom of the small stream on which we are now encamped about two miles south of the point where the old wagon trail via Fort Hall makes an angle and takes a northwesterly course. The bottom produces the finest quantities of grass and in great abundance. The water of the stream is cold and pure and abounds in spotted mountain trout and a variety of other small fish. [9]

Joel Palmer, who visited the fort in July of 1845, agreed that it was an excellent location. He said, "at this place, the bottoms are wide and covered with good grass . . . cottonwood timber in plenty and the stream abounds with trout." In fact, all of the recorded accounts of the location of Fort Bridger

Fort Bridger is located on an island created by branches of the Black's Fork.

seem very favorable because of the streams, the wide bottoms, the water, grass, willows, the fish in the streams, and the beautiful location of the snow-capped Uinta Mountains in the background.

However, the visitors were not as complimentary about the appearance of the fort as they were the general location. For example, Joel Palmer recorded:

This fort is owned by Bridger and Basquez. It is built of poles and dogwood mud. It is a shabby concern. There are about twenty five lodges of Indians or rather white trapper lodges occupied by their Indian wives. They have a good supply of robes, dressed deer, elk, and antelope skins, coats, pants, moccasins, other Indian fixins which they trade low for flour, pork, powder, lead, blankets, butcher knives, spirits, hats, ready made clothes, coffee, sugar, etc. They have a herd of cattle, twenty or thirty goats, and some sheep. [10]

John McBride, who visited Fort Bridger in July of 1846 with his family, wrote:

Pursuing our journey in three days more, we arrived at Fort Bridger so called by courtesy. It is only a camp where some fifty trappers were living in lodges.

12

The second Fort Bridger was built on this bluff overlooking the Black's Fork.

A single cabin of logs where the roof composed of willow brush covered with earth composed the fort. There was a large village of Indians of the Snake Tribe encamped here and a brisk traffic in dressed deer skins, buffalo robes, and logs went on during our stay with them which was half a day and the following night. The mountaineers and the Indians alike wanted to buy whiskey and brandy, but were not provided with this kind of merchandise. The next most desirable articles were coffee, sugars, soap, and flour. [11]

Edwin Bryant's impression of the fort was really no better. He simply said that there were two or three rudely constructed log cabins bearing but faint resemblance to habitable houses. But he did comment on the beauty of the location.

In summary, then, the famous Fort Bridger was established rather hastily in the summer of 1843 for the purpose of engaging in trade with the emigrants as well as the Indians, although to reach it travelers had to deviate some sixty to seventy miles from a direct line to Fort Hall. Very little was done to improve the post during its first three years. However, Bridger and Vasquez expected emigrants to continue to come to Fort Bridger since no other known route promised adequate water and forage.

2

Emigrant party along the Oregon Trail, from a painting by S. Jepperson.

Hastings' Cutoff brings prosperity to Fort Bridger

When Jim Bridger dictated his letter to Pierre Choteau and Company in December 1843, he remarked that he had good reason to feel that his new establishment "promised fairly" because of the number of emigrants that visited his post during the summer of 1843. The first of these emigrant parties included Overton Johnson, who reported:

On July 20, we met Messrs. Vasquez and Walker with a company of twenty or thirty mountain men coming down from the mountains where Messrs. Vasquez and Bridger had a small trading post among the Shoshone or Snake Indians. They were loaded with furs and skins which they were taking to the fort on the Platte where they supply themselves with such articles as they want for the Indian trade.[1]

A few days later, when Johnson's party arrived at Fort Bridger, they found it had been attacked by a band of Sioux who had killed a horse guard and two Snake Indians and had driven off a number of horses.

John Bordman, another emigrant, who arrived at Fort Bridger on 13 August 1843, also reported the difficulty with the Indians, stating that he had arrived expecting to stay ten or fifteen days in order to replenish their supply of meat, but was disappointed to learn that the Sioux and the Cheyenne Indians had been there and had run off all of the buffalo herd, killed three Snake Indians, and stolen sixty horses. Bordman reported that on Monday, August 14, while

15

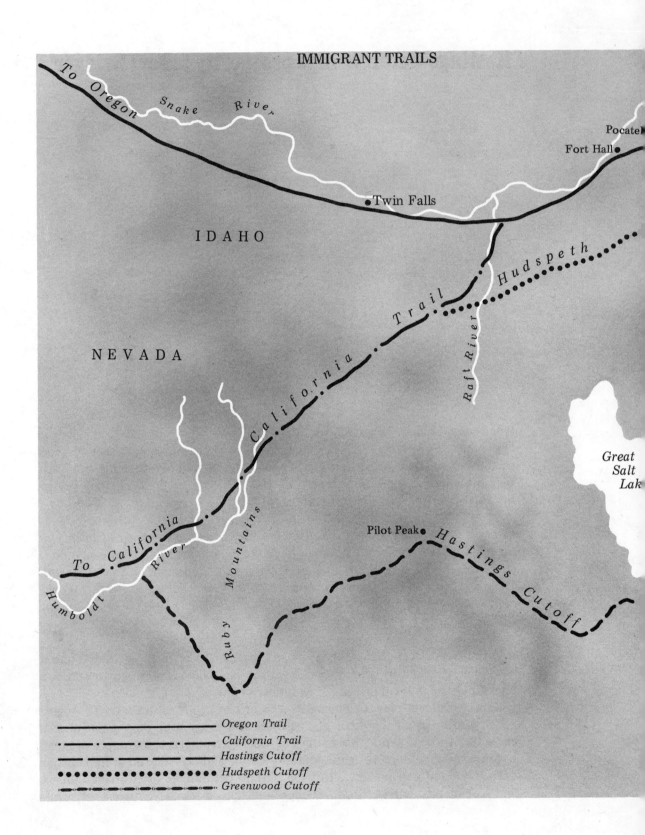

IMMIGRANT TRAILS

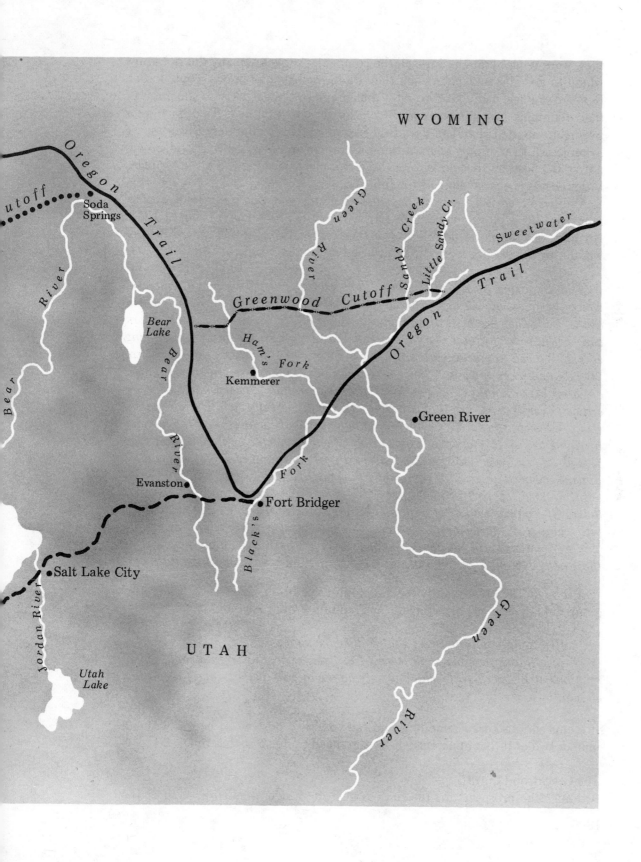

they were lying by at the fort, all the companies came up; many did not know where to go. The next day, when they discovered that a famous scout, Joseph Redford Walker, had agreed to pilot the Joseph B. Chiles' party to the point of the mountains in California, much of the tension vanished. Two days later Bordman reported they left Fort Bridger and started for the Bear River hoping to replenish their supply of meat there. Bordman also asserted that Bridger was not at the post, but had gone to St. Louis for blacksmithing and other supplies. Vasquez was in charge most of the time.[2]

Another interesting visitor, Theodore Talbot, who was with John C. Fremont and his exploring expedition, arrived at Fort Bridger on 30 August 1843. His diary gives a good description of the fort, and finally tells where Bridger was during his absence from the fort during this emigrant season.

Wed. 30th. Came nearly west along Black's Fork passing under the bluff on which Vasquez and Bridger's houses are built. We found them deserted and dismantled. They are built of logs, plastered with mud. We crossed Black's Fork and camped in the pretty valley which lies along either side of its winding course. We had not been here but a short time, when the guard gave the alarm "Les Indians, Les Indians." Sure enough, we could plainly see figures mounted on horseback coming dashing down the distant hills towards us. On more critical examination we thought that we could perceive white men among them. We were too far to see their countenances, but the dress and the manner of riding led us to make the supposition and their nearer approach soon confirmed it. Vasquez, with his gallant party of mountaineers and a band of Indians, came dashing into camps at full speed. Having exchanged salutations with the mad-cap party and the rest of Vasquez's Company, and the 15 or 20 lodges of Youta's who were with him having by this time come up, we all went into camp for the evening. Vasquez had just returned from hunting in the Youta Mountains. His partner old Jim Bridger, the most celebrated trapper of the Rocky Mts. has started with a party of forty men to trap on Wind River.[3]

Although Talbot was with the Fremont Expedition, apparently the entire group did not stop at Fort Bridger, for Fremont wrote that they:

. . . halted to noon on the river, a short distance above.
The Shoshonee woman took leave of us here, expecting to find some of her relations at Bridger's fort, which is only a mile or two distant, on a fort on this stream.[4]

It seems curious that Fremont would fail to visit a post when he was within a mile or two of it, but apparently he felt no need to do so at that time.

The Greenwood Cutoff
Although the prospects for the success of Fort Bridger seemed good after the

18

experience of the 1843 migration, the development of what is known as the Greenwood Cutoff in 1844 threatened the post's prosperity, if not its existence.

In 1844, as in 1843, Oregon rather than California was the chief attraction for emigrants, and the road from South Pass to Fort Hall was well marked by wagon wheels. From the Big Sandy encampment it ran southwest to the Green River, then south to Black's Fork, and up the stream some distance as far as Fort Bridger. However, Fort Bridger's location required emigrants to go sixty to seventy miles out of a direct route to Fort Hall and when a shortcut to Soda Springs was discovered, most of the westbound emigration of 1844, comprising some fifteen hundred persons, took it and bypassed Fort Bridger.

The shortcut, known as the Greenwood Cutoff and later as the Sublette Cutoff, left the old Oregon Trail before coming to Fort Bridger at a point east of the Little Sandy. It then ran nearly due west to the Big Sandy, and crossed a usually waterless desert to the Green River a few miles below present LaBarge, Wyoming. From the Green River a northwesterly route ran to the main road which runs between Fort Bridger and Soda Springs. Emigrants had been using the cutoff for at least five years when in 1849 Joseph E. Ware prepared his influential *Emigrant's Guide to California*, with a detailed description of the route, noting that some seventy miles could be saved by not passing Fort Bridger. However, there were warnings that the cutoff furnished little water.

When you cross the Dry or Little Sandy, instead of turning to the left and following the River, strike out across to the Big Sandy, twelve miles. If you get to the river along through the day, camp till near night. From the Big Sandy to Green River, a distance of thirty-five miles, there is not a drop of water. By starting from the Sandy at the cool of the day, you can get across easily by morning. Cattle can travel as far again by night as they can during the day, from the fact that the air is cool, and consequently they do not need water. Recollect, do not attempt to cross during the day.[5]

The continued description of the trail includes further information about supplies for the traveler:

You strike the Green river a few miles above a small stream that comes in from the northwest. After resting a day at Green river, keep a west, northwest course, to the branch, you strike it in about twelve miles by the trail; by keeping more west, you can reach it sooner. Follow it to the head, then strike across the high plain for the mountains, at the head of Thomas's Fork of the Bear River. Keep on the dividing ridge until you come near the Bear River Valley, then descend and cross down to the mouth of the Fork, when you find the main road. This is a fine road all the way; grass and fuel being plenty, and with the exception of the distance between the Sandy and Green River, there is fine water. By referring to large map, you can see that you save nearly five days travel by following what I have taken the liberty to call Sublette's Cutoff.

Apparently the first reference to the Greenwood Cutoff as such was by Edwin Bryant, who was at the Little Sandy on 14 July 1846, and wrote the following:

Our route this morning was across the plain some ten or twelve miles, when we struck the Big Sandy river. . . . The emigrant trail known as Greenwood's Cut-off, leaves the old trail via Fort Bridger to Fort Hall at this point. It is said to shorten the distance on the Fort Hall route to Oregon and California some fifty or sixty miles. The objection to the route is, that from Big Sandy to Green River, a distance of forty-five or fifty miles, there is no water.[6]

This cutoff threatened to ruin Bridger's emigrant trade, although the post was becoming the center of trade between mountain men and the Indians of the region. However, this type of trade was not especially profitable to the proprietors of the fort, and the post might have lost much of its importance in the westward migrations if a new route to California had not been conceived. The development of a new route, Hastings' Cutoff, greatly enhanced the growth and importance of Fort Bridger.

Lansford W. Hastings

Hastings was a young Ohio lawyer who in 1842 made the overland journey to Oregon. Dissatisfied with that country, he moved to California, where he readily grasped the tremendous possibilities open to an adventurer who could gather about himself a military force. Returning east in 1844, he published his *Emigrant's Guide to Oregon and California* in an attempt to lure emigrants to the sunny valleys of California. On his return trip to the west coast, Jim Bridger guided Hastings over a little known and difficult route from Fort Laramie to Fort Bridger in order to avoid hostile Indians on the warpath. Napoleon B. Smith, a member of Hastings' party, described the trip from Fort Laramie, where the Hastings party met Bridger, who had been detained from reaching his fort because of the Sioux-Snake wars. Bridger, who wanted to get back to his fort as much as Hastings and Smith wanted to reach California, proposed to the party that

. . . if they would accompany him, he would take them by a trail through the Wind River Mountains to Fort Bridger, by which the Country of the hostile Indians would be avoided. The proposition was accepted, so, after a stay of 10 days in Laramie, Smith and his companions left and guided by Bridger and the Frenchmen resumed their journey by the trail through the Wind River mountains. This trail was so rugged and wild that Smith believes to this day it is the

worst on the American Continent. Sometimes climbing precipitous mountains then down, down to a wild chasm, then assisting their animals with ropes over a precipice they would find themselves in a canion where sunlight never penetrated but on—on they went and after 20 days travel at length reached Fort Bridger. They had barely escaped encountering the Sioux, one party traveling on the South Side of Sweetwater mountain and the other on the North side.[7]

Hastings and Bridger reached Fort Bridger in October. Ignoring the advice of the experienced mountain man, Hastings continued his trip to California. It is not known what route he took, but it is likely that he followed the regular California trail rather than the cut-off trail he later devised. The season was late and the journey, even on a well-marked trail, was a foolhardy undertaking, indicating either Hastings' gross ignorance or his stubborn nature. However, he was fortunate enough to make it through the Sierras and arrived at Sutter's Fort on Christmas Day. It seems likely that he discussed his proposed route and cut-off with Bridger and alerted him to the possibility of increased trade in 1846. Hastings probably told Bridger of his plan to come back to South Pass in the early summer of 1846 and personally encourage emigrants to use his new route via Fort Bridger. He may have enlisted Bridger's aid in advertising the possibilities of the new cutoff.

Hastings' Cut-off

Ever since he first visited California in 1843, Hastings had been obsessed with the idea of taking California from Mexico and establishing it as an independent republic with himself as head. For such a project, settlers were necessary, and Hastings dedicated himself to attracting them to California. He concluded that he could reduce the distance to California by approximately 250 miles by advising wagon trains to leave the regular trail at Fort Bridger, "Thence bearing west southwest, to the Salt Lake; and thence continuing down to the Bay of St. Francisco." Unfortunately, he had never been over the cutoff himself and was guilty of encouraging emigrants with wagons to take this untried route.

He started east in April 1846 to wait along the trail and offer explicit advice to the emigrants. Fortunately, an old mountain man, James Clyman, was available to serve as his guide. Following the regular California Trail in reverse along the Humboldt, they branched off to cross the dreaded Great Salt Lake Desert, then to make their way south of the lake through the Wasatch Mountains to Fort Bridger, arriving there on the morning of 7 June 1846. Finding Fort Bridger deserted, Hastings continued on through South Pass and five days later camped on the North Platte River, where he encountered the first wagons of the 1846 emigration.

Hastings began contacting these emigrant groups, encouraging them to follow his new cutoff, and offering to lead them personally. Four groups decided to take his advice. Three of them made the trip successfully, but the

21

fourth, the Donner-Reed party, failed and experienced one of the great trage-
dies in the history of westward migration.

The first of the four groups, the Russell-Bryant party, consisted of ten
mounted men with pack animals, who arrived at Hastings' encampment (near
Fort Bridger) on July 16. Bryant, a Massachusetts-born Kentuckian, was a
newspaper editor traveling west for his health. Hearing of the cutoff, he wrote:

*July 18. We determined, this morning, to take the new route, via the south end
of the Great Salt Lake. Mr. Hudspeth—who with a small party, on Monday, will
start in advance of the emigrant companies which intend traveling by this
route, for the purpose of making some further explorations—has volunteered to
guide us as far as the Salt Plains, a day's journey west of the Lake.*[8]

These ten men on horseback were successful in crossing through the Wasatch
Mountains via Weber Canyon, but were convinced that wagon trains could
never make it, especially those with large, heavy wagons like those of the
Donner-Reed party. Bryant rode back up the Weber near the present site of
Croyden and left a note advising the Donner-Reed party to go further north to
the Ogden River valley, but the Donners had been directed by Hastings to go
another way and did not know of Bryant's efforts in their behalf.

Two other parties were successful in taking wagons through the Weber
Canyon route, however. The Harlan-Young party, with Hastings as their guide,
left Fort Bridger on July 20, closely followed by a party of Swiss emigrants led
by Heinrich Reinhard. Both parties arrived in Salt Lake Valley without undue
hardship, but Hastings was convinced that the Donner party, which had arrived
at Fort Bridger on 27 July 1846, too late to join the Harlan-Young group,
could not get their wagons through the narrow, rocky Weber Canyon. Hastings
left a note near present-day Hennefer, Utah, advising them to send men on
horseback through the Wasatch Mountains to contact him on the shores of the
Great Salt Lake and he would guide them over a more feasible route.

The ill-fated Donner group had decided to take the cutoff because of
Hastings' advertising and his promise to lead them. Eliza P. Donner Houghton,
writing at the Little Sandy, said that her father and others deliberated over the
new route to California, but were led to take it by "An Open Letter," which
had been delivered to their company on July 17, by Lansford W. Hastings,
author of *Travel Among the Rocky Mountains Through Oregon and California.*
It was dated and addressed, "at the Headquarters of the Sweetwater: To all
California emigrants now on the road," and intimated that on account of the
war between Mexico and the United States, "the government of California
would probably oppose the entrance of American emigrants to its territory,"
and urged those on the way to California to concentrate their numbers and
strength and to take the new and better route which he had explored from Fort
Bridger, by way of the south end of Salt Lake. The letter emphasized the

22

Lansford Hastings, enigmatic California pioneer, promoted the Hastings cutoff.

23

statement that this new route was nearly two hundred miles shorter than the old one by way of Fort Hall "and the headwaters of Ogden River (Humboldt)" and that Hastings would remain at Fort Bridger "to give further information and to conduct the emigrants through to the settlement." Mrs. Houghton stated that her father was elected captain of the company, and from that time on it was known as the Donner party. Five days later the Donner party reached Fort Bridger, and were informed by Hastings' agent "that he had gone forward as pilot to a large emigrant train, but had left instructions that all later arrivals should follow his trail."[9]

On July 31, one of Donner's partners, James Reed, in a letter to James Keyes, stated:

Fort Bridger, one hundred miles from the Eutaw or Great Salt Lake, July 31, 1846

We have arrived here safe with the loss of two yoke of my best oxen. They were poisoned by drinking water in a little creek called Dry Sandy, situated between the Green Spring in the Pass of the Mountains, and Little Sandy. The water was standing in puddles. . . . I have replenished my stock by purchasing from Messrs. Vasquez and Bridger, two very excellent and accommodating gentlemen, who are the proprietors of this trading post. The new road, or Hastings' Cutoff, leaves the Fort Hall road here, and is said to be a saving of 350 or 400 miles in going to California, and a better route. There is, however, or thought to be, one stretch of 40 miles without water; but Hastings and his party, are out a-head examining for water, or for a route to avoid this stretch. I think that they cannot avoid it, for it crosses an arm of the Eutaw Lake, now dry. Mr. Bridger, and other gentlemen here, who have trapped that country say that the Lake has receded from the tract of country in question. There is plenty of grass which we can cut and put into the waggons, for our cattle while crossing it. . . . Mr. Bridger informs me that the route we design to take, is a fine level road, with plenty of water and grass, with the exception before stated. It is estimated that 700 miles will take us to Capt. Sutter's Fort, which we hope to make in seven weeks from this day.

I want to inform the emigration that they can be supplied with fresh cattle by Messrs. Vasquez and Bridger . . . and they can be relied on for doing business honorably and fairly . . . Vasquez and Bridger are the only fair traders in these parts.[10]

The praise that Reed had in his letter for Bridger and Vasquez was later changed to contempt, since Reed put considerable blame on them for the Donner tragedy. His reason was that the letters written by Bryant to his "friends in the emigrant parties in the rear" on July 18 and left at Fort Bridger were never delivered. Whether this is true or not, it seems certain that Bridger and Vasquez were active in promoting Hastings' Cutoff. It meant the difference

24

James Reed, with his wife Margaret, was a leader of the ill-fated Donner party.

between success and failure of their trading establishment. Of course, they could not know that the Donner-Reed party would take a full month to go from Fort Bridger to Salt Lake Valley, and would eventually be marooned by an early snowstorm in the high Sierras, leading to the tragic death of over half of the eighty-seven emigrants. The remainder survived only after experiencing months of extreme cold and hunger and near starvation. They avoided total starvation only by eating human flesh.

Despite this tragedy, Hastings' Cutoff brought new prosperity to Fort Bridger, and the success of the War with Mexico made the future especially bright. It seemed certain that California would be acquired by the United States, and emigration to that region would certainly increase. The owners of Fort Bridger could not have anticipated how soon nor at how great a rate the transcontinental migration would increase for great quantities of gold were soon to be discovered in California.

Another development was taking place that would also bring thousands of emigrants to Fort Bridger. This was the mass migration of the Mormons, not to California but to the valley of the Great Salt Lake, and it would change the history of Fort Bridger dramatically.

3

Gold seekers were among the many travelers who stopped to rest at Fort Bridger.

Mormon pioneers and California argonauts

The emigrant trains that visited Fort Bridger in 1846 seemed sizable when compared with preceding years, but it was a mere trickle compared with the flood of emigrants that came through the area in 1847, 1848, and 1849. Two important events in the history of the American West were responsible for this development. The first was the decision of the Mormons to leave their homes in Illinois and Iowa and migrate to the Great Basin, and the second was the gold rush to California in 1849.

The Mormon migration was a sizable one. Approximately fifteen thousand Mormons were forced to leave their homes in and around Nauvoo, Illinois, early in 1846. Somewhat disorganized at first, they moved slowly across Iowa and finally stopped at Council Bluffs on the east bank of the Missouri River. It was here that they accepted a government invitation to supply a battalion of men to march to California as a part of General Stephen A. Kearney's Army of the West. The departure of these men forced the Mormon leaders to abandon their plan to go to the Great Basin in 1846, and they spent the winter of 1846-47 at Council Bluffs and across the river at Winter Quarters, a few miles north of present-day Omaha, Nebraska.

Early in April, 1847, the Mormon leader, Brigham Young, led a pioneer band of 143 men, three women, and two children west from Winter Quarters—the vanguard of a well-organized mass migration to the Great Basin from various parts of the United States, Canada, Great Britain, Europe, Australia, and the Pacific Islands.

This artist's imaginative drawing shows the rustic simplicity of the early fort.

On 28 June 1847 the Mormon pioneer party, migrating to the Rocky Mountains, met James Bridger and two Frenchmen, who were traveling from Fort Bridger to Fort Laramie. Each party being anxious to interview the other, they camped together for the night on the Little Sandy. Bridger had dinner as the guest of Brigham Young, and talked far into the night with him and the apostles of the Church who accompanied him. It was during this conversation that Bridger criticized the Fremont maps the Mormons were using to aid them. He was also reputed to have offered to pay $1,000 for the first ear of corn raised in Salt Lake Valley, but there is some question as to what the old mountain man really said on that occasion.[1]

Descriptions of Fort Bridger in 1847-48

The Mormons reached Fort Bridger on 7 July 1847, and many of their diaries contain excellent descriptions of the fort. William Clayton made reference to Fort Bridger on July 3, when he wrote, "At night Pres. Young gave the brethren some instructions about trading at Fort Bridger and advised them to be wise, etc." Clayton's journal related that Bridger told Brigham Young that his blacksmith shop at the fort had been destroyed by Indians on an earlier raid and that they would have to use their own equipment. Several of the diaries made reference to blacksmithing during the layover at the fort.

On July 7, upon reaching the fort, Clayton reported the distance to be 397

Situated on the Mormon Trail, Fort Bridger was a supply station for emigrants.

miles from Fort John, near Fort Laramie. The company camped half a mile beyond the fort, having traveled seventeen miles for the day. Clayton describes the natural surroundings:

The grass is very plentiful in this neighborhood and much higher than we have generally seen it. The whole region seems filled with rapid streams all bending their way to the principal fork. They doubtless originate from the melting of the snow on the mountains and roar down their cobbly beds till they join Black's Fork.

Then he continues with a description of the fort itself:

Bridger's fort is composed of two double log houses about forty feet long each and joined by a pen for horses about ten feet high constructed by placing poles upright in the ground close together, which is all the appearance of a fort in sight. There are several Indian lodges close by and a full crop of young children playing around the door. These Indians are said to be of the Snake tribe, the Utahs inhabiting beyond the Mountains. The latitude of Fort Bridger is 41° 19" 13' and its height above the level of the sea according to Elder Pratt's observation is 6,665 ft. It is doubtless a very cold region and little calculated for farming purposes.[2]

29

Wilford Woodruff, writing on the same day, did not give the detailed description of the fort that Clayton gave but did give some interesting comments on the merits of fishing the small streams by the fort in comparison to other trading posts. Before they reached the campground beyond the fort, he reported they "crossed more than a dozen trout brooks, the water running swiftly but clear, with hard, gravelly bottoms." He also noticed "the whole region of country up and down these streams was covered with grass knee deep." Some of the Mormons had success catching brook trout, so as the company was to spend the next day at the fort, Woodruff "calculated on a day of fishing." In the style of a true sportsman, he wrote:

As soon as I had my breakfast next morning I rigged up my fishing rod that I had brought with me from Liverpool, fixed my reel line and artificial fly, and went to one of the brooks close by to try my luck. The men at the fort said that there were but few trout in the streams and a good many of the brethren were already at the creeks with their rods, trying their skill, baiting with fresh meat and grasshoppers, but not one was catching any. . . . I fished two or three hours during the morning and evening and caught twelve in all. One half of them would weigh three-fourths of a pound each, while all the rest of the camp did not catch three pounds in all, which was taken as proof that the artificial fly is far the best to fish with.

Later, he reported his encounter with Bridger's trading post:

In the afternoon I went to Bridger's house and traded off my flintlock rifle for four buffalo robes which were large, nice and well dressed. I found things generally at least one-third higher than I had ever known them at any other trading post I ever saw in America.[3]

One of the most detailed Mormon descriptions of the fort in 1847 was given on July 7 in the diary of Orson Pratt who was traveling in advance of the main party and making scientific observations. After recording his crossing of Black's Fork River, he describes:

Nine Indian lodges stood a few rods distant, occupied by the families of the trappers and hunters, who have taken squaws for wives. Some few half-breed children were seen playing about their lodges. Bridger's trading post is situated half a mile due west of these lodges on an island. The main camp having arrived, we passed over four branches of Black's Fork, without any road but a foot-path. Three quarters of a mile brought us to the door of Bridger's. We here turned to the south, and crossing three more branches camped within half a mile of the post. Black's Fork is here broken up into quite a number of rapid streams, forming a number of islands, all containing 700 or 800 acres of most excellent grass, with considerable timber, principally cottonwood and willow. Bridger's post consists of two adjoining log houses, dirt roofs, and a small picket yeard of logs set in the ground, about 8 feet high. The number of men, squaws, and half-breed children in these houses and lodges, may be about 50 or 60. . . . Mosquitoes very numerous and troublesome.[4]

Pratt commented about the cold nights even in the middle of the summer, saying, "The morning is cold. Ice formed during the night, which however, was soon melted by the rising sun."

George A. Smith wrote the following description of the fort:

Bridger's Fort consists of two long, low, rough cabins built in the form of an L with a small enclosure for stock built of upright poles. The surrounding country was beautiful, but the fort itself was an unpretentious place.[5]

From the descriptions left in 1847 it is evident that the fort had remained basically the same since its construction in 1843. It would appear that Bridger and Vasquez were satisfied that the fort was meeting their needs during the time spent there.

Two companies comprising 177 people, including the majority of the Mormon leaders, returned from Salt Lake Valley to Winter Quarters in August 1847. Several of them made journal entries in reference to passing or spending the night near the fort in late August or early September. As in July on their westward trek, the Mormons did not find Bridger or Vasquez at the fort as they traveled east. In September, two other large companies of westbound Mormon emigrants, totalling approximately 1,500 souls, reached Fort Bridger. Many of these people described the fort but did not give any additional information.

The Mormon migration of 1848, which was much larger than in 1847, passed the fort, and the people wrote descriptions and comments. The majority of the accounts are duplications of the 1847 descriptions of the fort and its setting; however, there were two new items mentioned in the diaries which merit consideration. According to several diaries, Louis Vasquez was present at the fort during the emigration of 1848, although Bridger was absent as usual. Secondly, it was noted that Bridger and Vasquez had built onto the fort since the fall of 1847. John D. Lee recorded the following about the new additions:

Cloudy and rained till about 9 and about 10 J.D. Lee again resumed his travel. Road slippery. Traveled 14 ms. to Ft. Bridger and Encamped. H. C. Kimbal stapped 4 ms. back, but several smaul cos, of his camp lay at or near Bridger, Water pure and clear; feed first rate and wood sufficient for camping purposes. The FT consists of 8 Block Houses and a smaul Enclosure picketed in. Land exceeding rich, grass durable winter and summer, all though there is Frost every month of the year.[6]

It is very possible the new additions, six log cabins, were built to accommodate Vasquez's family which he had brought from St. Louis in 1847. Due to the emigrant season it was not until the fall of 1847 and spring of 1848 that Vasquez and Bridger could have found time to construct the new log buildings. Also, Bridger's first wife had died in 1846. The exact date of his second marriage is not available but it is known that his second wife died on 4 July 1849. It is possible the new buildings were erected in 1847 and 1848 for the brides of both Bridger and Vasquez. It might be conjectured that the news of the discovery of gold in California in January 1848 may have been responsible for the building activity, but it does not seem likely. Samuel Brannan, the young Mormon leader in San Francisco, did not make his dramatic announcement of the discovery of gold until April, and it took some time for the news to reach Bridger. Unfortunately, it is not known when such news arrived nor what immediate impact it had upon the proprietors of Fort Bridger.

However, Willard Richards, who was in charge of a large company of Mormons en route to the Great Salt Lake, arrived at Fort Bridger on 5 October 1848, and made no mention of an anticipated gold rush. The entry in his diary is very interesting because it helps support the idea that Vasquez managed the trading post with Bridger absent most of the time. It also suggested the beginning of Mormon influence at the fort. Richards wrote, "... company traveled 8¼ miles to Fort Bridger. Arrived at 2 PM. Vasquez in charge of the fort. He had discharged his other hands and had engaged two or three Mormons."[7]

It should be noted that the coming of the Mormons was a mixed blessing as far as Fort Bridger was concerned. The Donner experience did not encourage emigrants to risk the cutoff, but with the establishment of Salt Lake City in 1847 the route became much more desirable. Not only was there now a city which provided rest and supplies on the Hastings' Cutoff (called the Mormon Trail after 1847), but Mormons had developed a new southern route to California, by-passing the Sierra Mountains and the difficulties that led to the Donner tragedy. The establishment of the Mormons in the Great Basin brought many thousands of emigrants, both Mormon and non-Mormon, in contact with Fort Bridger. However, the Mormon settlements also took away from the fort the majority of the trade, including Indian, and placed it in the hands of the Salt Lake merchants. There was little reason for a Mormon en route to Salt Lake to buy supplies at Fort Bridger when his destination was only one hundred miles away. And why should the non-Mormon emigrant en route to California via the Great Salt Lake trade at the fort when both quantity and quality were better in the Mormon settlement? Ironically, then, even though the coming of the Mormons brought more emigrants to Fort Bridger, which certainly brought some degree of trade to the owners, the fort suffered economically from the loss of trade to Salt Lake City.

Added to this disadvantage was the exceptionally cold winter of 1848-49, which was unusually hard at Fort Bridger. The previous winter had been very

Rare photograph of Brigham Young, leader of the Mormons; taken in 1847.

mild, with the livestock grazing around the fort the entire winter. On 16 April 1849, Thomas S. Williams, returning from Fort Bridger, reported that "the winter had been severe there, and the traders at that place had suffered almost starvation, having lived on their cattle, which had parished." The snow was reported by Williams to be "50 ft. deep drifts at Yellow Creek and 15 feet on the plain at Cache Cave." However, within a few weeks, the first of thousands of gold seekers who stopped at Fort Bridger en route to California in 1849 and the years following helped the owners recoup their losses.

The Gold Rush and Its Influence

Very few non-Mormon emigrants had visited Fort Bridger in 1847-48, but the discovery of gold in California late in 1848 had a great impact on the future of the trading post. Since the Mormon Trail via Fort Bridger and the Great Salt Lake was the most direct route to California, it was more frequently traveled. The flood of prospectors and merchants traveling east and west increased the business at the fort. One evidence of the increase of emigrants was reported by a Mormon traveler who reported that "the feed between Fort Laramie and Fort Bridger was completely gone."

Bridger and Vasquez soon realized the potential of the 1849 migration. Knowing that some travelers en route to California would take the Sublette Cutoff to Fort Hall, they tried to persuade them to take the Mormon Trail via Fort Bridger by setting up a branch of their establishment at the last crossing of the Sweetwater about one hundred and fifteen miles from Fort Bridger. The diaries of the forty-niners indicate the branch post was there from about June 9 to July 1.

Peter Decker, who reached the last crossing of the Sweetwater on Friday, 15 June 1849, wrote concerning the temporary trading post:

Reached the sweetwater crossed it and camped on bottom, found several traders with skins, robes, horses and mules trading with Emigrants, they are a sharp set of traders, Mr. Vasquez and Bridger. These men have habits like Indians, long hair, skin clothing, quick perception and active motions. Rather intelligent men . . . have 3 or 4 lodges here saw several filthy looking children and squaws. Bacon worth $10.00, offered good robe for 1 gal whisky.[8]

It is not known how many travelers stopped at Fort Bridger in 1849, but they must have numbered in the hundreds. Dr. Leonard Arrington, author of *Great Basin Kingdom*, estimates that ten to fifteen thousand gold seekers passed through Salt Lake City in 1849 and 1850, bringing an economic boom to the young community. It seems safe to assume that most, if not all, of the gold seekers who followed the Mormon Trail through the Wasatch Mountains had stopped at Fort Bridger for supplies and directions before attempting to negotiate the mountain road. And, of course, all the gold seekers did not reach California in 1849 and 1850. There was a steady stream of people visiting Fort Bridger during the next few years on their way to seek the riches of California.

Another event took place in 1849 that helped increase the patronage of Fort Bridger. It was early that year that a band of Cherokee Indians en route to California "came north along the Front Ranges of the Rockies to the Cache la Poudre, then went via the Laramie Plains and Bitter Creek to strike the Salt Lake Road east of Fort Bridger." This was the opening of the Cherokee Trail. It became one of the major routes for emigrants in 1849 traveling via the present site of Denver to intersect the Oregon and new Overland routes.

The Overland route, which ran in almost a direct line from Fort Laramie to Fort Bridger, was being traveled in 1849 and was described by John Wilson.

There is a road already opened by partial travel almost in a direct line from Fort Bridger to Fort Laramie which crosses Green River below the mouth of Hams [Black] Fork and perhaps above the mouth of Marys [Yampa] river and thence pretty directly across the mountains to one of the forks of Laramie river and thence down to Fort Laramie which will cut off more than 150 miles in the distance. . . . Mr. Vasquez says it is a much better road and passes the Rocky Mountains by a pass considerably lower than the South Pass and affords a far better supply of both water and grass.[9]

This route was favored by many emigrants who visited Fort Bridger on their way to California.

4

Washakie, the Shoshone chief for sixty years, was important in the fort's history.

Civilization closes in on Fort Bridger

The Mormon colonization of Salt Lake Valley just one hundred miles from Fort Bridger, and the Treaty of Guadaloupe Hidalgo which ended the war with Mexico and added all of Upper California, including Fort Bridger, to the United States, led to the first attempt to bring civil government to the region. Prior to this time the owners of Fort Bridger had been free from any type of governmental control from Mexico or the United States.

The first government to claim jurisdiction over the post was the Mormon "State of Deseret," organized in March 1849. Although it was never officially recognized by the federal government, the fully organized State of Deseret functioned until it was superceded by the Utah territorial government in the spring of 1851.

As early as 28 January 1850 an ordinance providing for the location of counties and precincts in the newly organized "State of Deseret" was passed. Section 16 provided that "There shall be a precinct named Bridger Precinct at Black's Fork including the settlement of all white inhabitants in that region between the Bear and the Green River and within the limits of this state until otherwise provided by law." A census taken by the State of Deseret officials indicated that there were twenty-two males and twenty-four females living in the Green River or Bridger Precinct at that time.

Creation of the Utah Territory
The Territory of Utah was created on 9 September 1850, but it was considerably later when the presidential list of officials received the sanction of the

Senate, and almost a full year before all of the new officers assembled in the territory. Brigham Young received word that he had been appointed governor and superintendent of Indian affairs of the Territory of Utah in January, and took office on 3 February 1851.

An act extending the Intercourse Act of 1834 to Utah Territory was passed which provided three sub-agents to help conduct the Indian affairs in the territory. On 2 July 1851 Governor Young ordered the territory divided into three agencies: the Pauvan Agency, the Uintah Agency and the Parowan Agency. The Uintah Agency was to include all the Snake, Shoshone, Uintah, and Yampa Indians within the territory, and all other tribes within the territory east of the eastern rim of the Great Basin. Consequently, Fort Bridger, located within the political boundaries of the newly created Uintah Agency, came under the direction of Brigham Young as governor and Indian superintendent. This dual role led Brigham Young to investigate Bridger's activity with the Indians.

Prior to the organization of Utah Territory, the Indian affairs had been handled by Indian agent John Wilson, who arrived at Fort Bridger on 21 August 1849, the day after Stansbury left the fort with Bridger as his guide. Wilson, writing to the Commissioner of Indian Affairs from Fort Bridger, seemed favorably impressed with Bridger and Vasquez when he reported:

Sir: We arrived here yesterday. Messrs. Vasquez and Bridger are the proprietors, and have resided here and in these mountains for more than twenty-five years. They are engaged as traders, belonging to the American Fur Company. They are gentlemen of integrity and intelligence, and can be fully relied on in relation to any statement they make in regard to the different tribes, claims, boundaries, and other information in relation to the Utah and Sho-shonies tribe, and a small band of Bannocks, as they have during all their residence, been engaged in trade with them.[1]

Wilson also gave a very detailed account of the different tribes and the boundaries of their domain, number of lodges and the names of the leading chiefs. He reported that because of the Mormon settlement and popularity of the Mormon Trail, all the game had been driven away from the Fort Bridger area and it was a problem that must be dealt with. Wilson felt that it would be wise to meet at Fort Bridger with the Indians in the area as soon as possible, and to take steps to regulate some system of intercourse with the Indians.

Later, writing from Salt Lake City on September 4, Wilson reported that upon approval by the "department" he would ". . . next summer hold a grand counsel of the two nations (Shoshonee and Bannock) at Fort Bridger when I will endeavor to carry out these or such other views as the department shall direct me with these two nations. . . ." He felt ". . . Fort Bridger to be the most proper place" to meet with the Indians,

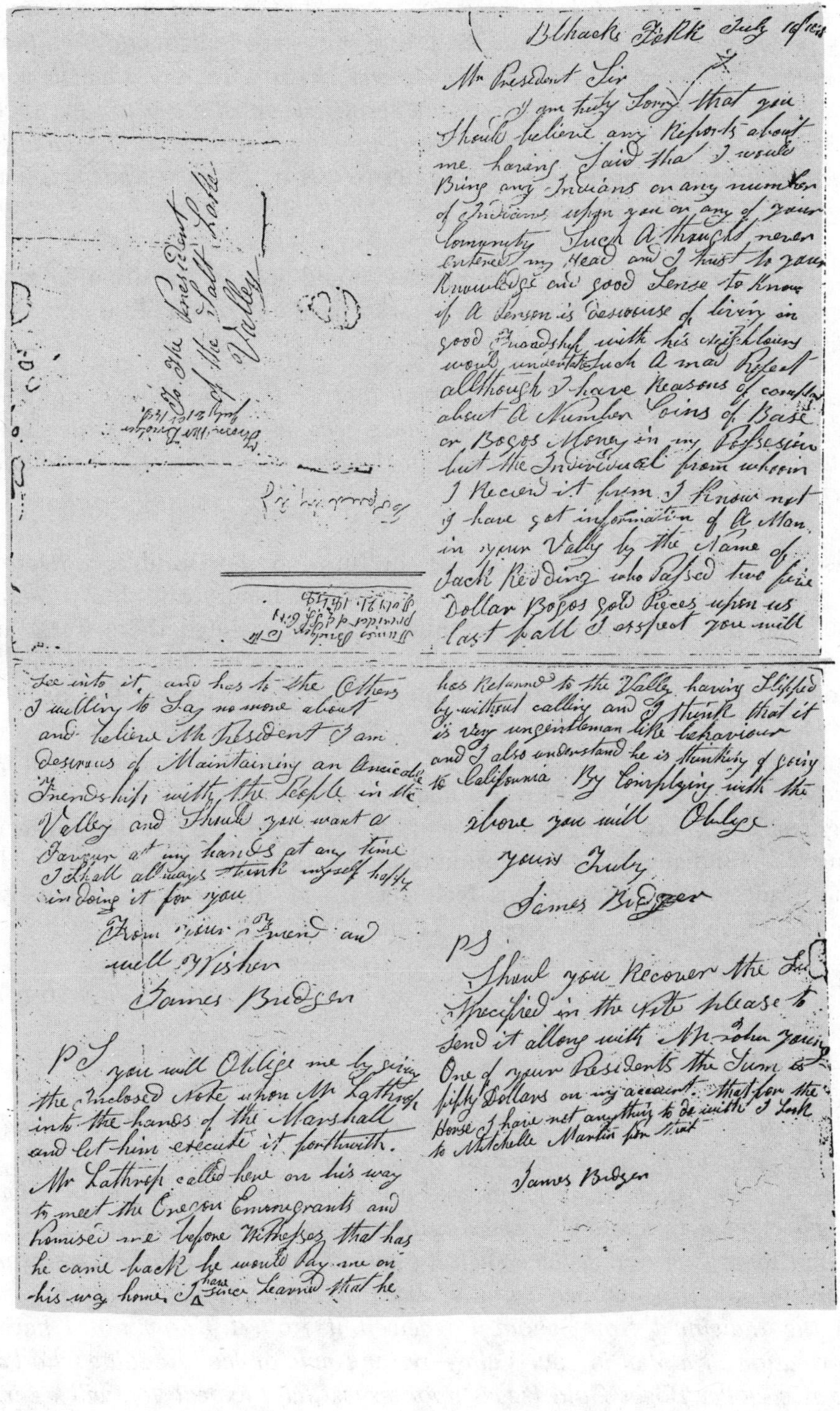

Blacks Fork July 19 1848

Mr President Sir

I am truly Sorry that you Should believe any Reports about me haveing Said that I would Bring any Indians or any number of Indians upon you or any of your community Such A thought never entered my Head and I trust to your Knowledge and good Sense to know if A person is desirous of living in good Friendship with his Neighbours would undertake Such A war Respect allthough I have Reasons of complaint about A Number Coins of Base or Bogos Money in my Possession but the Individual from whoom I Recived it from I know not I have got information of A Man in your Valley by the Name of Jack Redding who Passed two five Dollar Bogos gold Peices upon us last fall I expect you will

[second page left column]

See into it and has to the Others I willing to Say no more about and believe Mr President I am Desirous of Maintaining an Amicable Friendship with the People in the Valley and Should you want a Favour at my hands at any time I Shall allways think myself happy in doing it for you

From your Friend and well Wisher

James Bridger

PS You will Oblige me by giving the inclosed Note upon Mr Lathrop into the hands of the Marshall and let him execute it forthwith Mr Lathrop called here on his way to meet the Oregon Emmegrants and promised me before Witnesses that has he came back he would pay me on his way home I have since learnd that he

[second page right column]

has Returned to the Valley having Slipped by without calling and I think that it is very ungentleman like behaviour and I also understand he is thinking of going to California By Complying with the above you will Oblige

Yours Truly
James Bridger

PS

Should you Recover the Sum Specified in the note please to Send it allong with Mr John Young one of your Presidents the Sum is fifty Dollars on my account that for the Horse I have not anything to do with I Look to Mitchelle Martin for that

James Bridger

[address panel, left]
To the President of the Salt Lake Valley

Letter dictated by Jim Bridger to Mormon leader Brigham Young, 21 July 1848.

39

... as it is unquestionably the easiest of access to them and besides it has for a long period been the principle place, where they have traded; and then the vast valleys of the finest grass on the very many fine small streams and brooks in that vicinity which abound in fur makes it the most fit place for such an assemblage and then there are no settlements of whites in the vicinity to corrupt them with spirits and other things to annoy, for such traders as may be there will be subject to the law.[2]

Wilson also suggested that Fort Bridger should become the site of a principal agency for the Indians and also be the location of a leading military post of the mountains. Wilson revealed that he had

... spoken to Washikick, the principal chief of the Sho-sho-nie and that he highly approved the plan. Major Vasquez, was also in favor of the plan and would help in contacting the Indians in the area for the meeting to follow the next summer at the fort.[3]

Wilson's recommendations concerning the future of Fort Bridger in relation to the Indian problems were not original. Both Stansbury and J. W. Gunnison recommended basically the same thing. Stansbury stated there were "many reasons for establishing a military post west of the mountains and that Fort Bridger," in his opinion, "offered a number of advantages for the location of such a garrison."[4] Gunnison went so far as to recommend both a fort and an agency and suggested that Bridger be made the Indian agent. This plan might have been followed if Fort Bridger had not been located in Utah Territory, but Brigham Young saw Bridger in quite a different light. He felt that Bridger was lying to the Indians about the Mormons and to the Mormons about the Indians. That Bridger was aware of this feeling is shown in a letter dictated by the mountain man to President Brigham Young:

July 16th 1848

Blhacks Fork
Mr. President Sir

I am truly sorry that you should believe any reports about me having said that I would bring any number of Indians upon you and any of your community. Such a thought never entered my head and I trust to your knowledge and good sense to know if a person is desirous of living in good friendship with his neighbors would undertake such a mad project. Although I have reasons of complaint about a number Coins of Base or Bogos Money in my possession but the Individual from whom I received it from I Know not I have got information of a Man in your Valley by the Name of Jack Redding who Passed two five Dollar Bogos Gold Pieces upon us last fall I expect you will see into it and has to the Others I willing to Say no more about and believe Mr. President

40

I am Desirous of Maintaining an Amieable Friendship with the People in the Valley and Should you want a Favour at my hands at any time I Shall allways think myself happy in doing it for you

> *From your Friend and*
> *Well Wisher*
> *James Bridger   X*

PS you will Oblige me by giving the Enclosed note upon Mr. Lathrop into the hands of the Marshall and let him execute it forthwith. Mr. Lathrop called here on his way to meet the Oregon Emigrants and promised me before Witnesses that has he came back he would Pay me on his way home. I have since Learned that he has returned to the Valley having Slipped by without calling and I think that it is very ungentleman like behavior and I also understand he is thinking of going to California

> *By complying with the above you*
> *will Oblige Yours Truly*
> *James Bridger*

PS Should you Recover the Sum Specified in the Note please to send it allong with Mr. John Young One of your Presidents the Sum is fifty Dollars on my account. that for the Horse I have not anything to do with I look to Mitchelle Martin for that

> *James Bridger* [5]

Bridger and Vasquez demonstrated further evidence of friendship when on 9 April 1849 the Church leaders received a letter of warning from them asserting that the Indians were badly disposed against the whites and that "Old Elk and Walkara were erging attack on the settlement of saints in Utah Valley." A month later, Young received from Vasquez a letter stating that Barney Ward and two other men had been trading with the Bannock Indians, and that "an Indian with two horses and some bear skins left the village to go with them but he was subsequently found murdered below the junction of Ham's and Black's Fork."[6] Vasquez wished to know how many horses Ward had brought into the valley, and stated "that the band of Indians were incensed, and talked of coming to the valley to war upon the white."

In a rather curious reaction to this correspondence, President Brigham Young commented, "I believe I know that Old Bridger is death on us, and if he knew 400,000 Indians were coming against us, and any man were to let us know, he would cut his throat." Young revealed his prejudice when he wrote "Vasquez is a different sort of man. I believe Bridger is watching every movement of the Mormons, and reporting to Thomas Benton at Washington."[7]

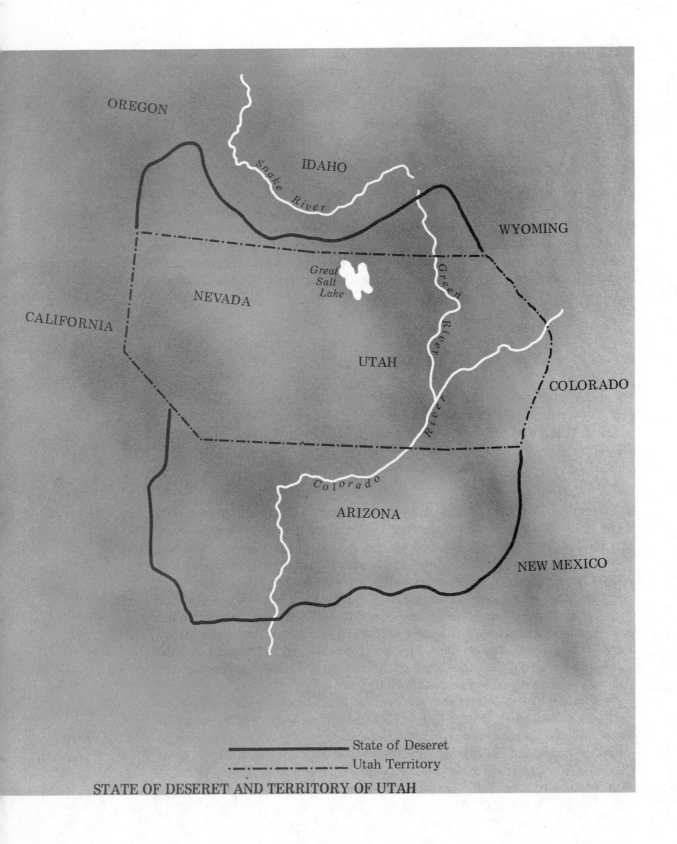

OREGON

IDAHO

Snake River

WYOMING

Great
Salt
Lake

Green River

NEVADA

CALIFORNIA

UTAH

COLORADO

River

Colorado

ARIZONA

NEW MEXICO

———— State of Deseret
—·—·— Utah Territory

STATE OF DESERET AND TERRITORY OF UTAH

In a meeting a week later Brigham Young said that he felt "Bridger and the other mountaineers were the real cause of the Indians being incensed against the Saints, if they really were incensed."

Thomas L. "Peg-leg" Smith added to Brigham Young's suspicions when he reported:

. . . that he did not think Bridger and Vasquez had killed the Indian, for those persons were not brave enough, but they might have caused it to be done, to bring on a fuss between the Indians and our people, Bridger and Vasquez being jealous of them trading with the Indians.[8]

The Indians did not attack the Utah Valley in 1849 as Bridger and Vasquez had anticipated, but it seems quite possible that the proprietors of Fort Bridger were sincere in warning the Mormons despite Brigham Young's opinion of Bridger.

Indian Agent Wilson's recommendation that the Indians in the Fort Bridger area be given government help was taken seriously by the Uintah Agency of the Utah Territorial Indian Superintendency. There is little question that the condition of the Indians in the Bridger area in 1850 was pitiful. Since the erection of the fort, the condition of the Shoshone and Bannock Indians had steadily deteriorated. The white man, coming over the Oregon Trail, had been driving away or slaughtering the buffalo and other game so necessary to the Indian economy. It was very apparent by 1850 that the federal government needed to assist the Indians if they were to survive. During the next several years Fort Bridger became a very important meeting point for the Indians and the government officials in carrying out the program set up by the commissioner of Indian affairs in Washington, D.C.

Unfortunately, agents Holeman and Day were in constant disagreement with the Mormons. Their letters to the commissioner of Indian affairs were full of statements blaming the Mormons for the majority of the Indian problems in the Utah Territory and quoting Indian leaders concerning their distrust of the Mormons. They may have been reflecting their own feelings, for agent Holeman claimed that most nonmembers (gentiles) in the Salt Lake area could not trust the post office with their mail. Holeman wrote:

It is believed by many that there is an examination of all letters, coming and going—in order that they may ascertain what is said of them, and by whom it is said. This opinion is so strong, that all communications touching their character and conduct, are either sent to Fort Bridger or Fort Laramie, there to be mailed.[9]

A different point of view was expressed by sub-agent Stephen B. Rose who wrote to Superintendent Young on 31 March 1852 and indicated that the Indians' negative attitude toward the Mormons in the Fort Bridger area was not the fault of the Mormons as Holeman and Day suggested but that of the trappers and traders along the Green River. Rose wrote:

I would suggest the propriety of calling the attention of the Department to a number of French Canadian Traders settled upon the Green River and in the Neighborhood of Fort Bridger who are constantly trading with the Indians although they have been notified to the contrary they have had a number of the different tribes together this winter and made a number of speaches to them endeavoring to prejudice them against the peaceful inhabitants of this valley.[10]

A study of the letters written by Holeman to Indian Commissioner Luke Lea in Washington reveals that much of Holeman's information concerning the Indians' attitude toward the Mormons was obtained from Bridger. As indicated earlier, Brigham Young was suspicious of Bridger's attitudes and activities and thought that he had told the Mormons one thing and the Indians another. A good example of this is recorded in Brigham Young's journal under the date of 4 September 1853: "30 of Washakie's men arrived at Great Salt Lake and told Brigham Young that Bridger had told Washakie that he Young would kill him if he went to Great Salt Lake. Washakie turned back to the Sweetwater and sent his men."[11] If this is a correct report by the Indians, it may be that Bridger was purposely giving out incorrect information.

It appears that both the Mormon leaders and the Indian agents were operating on rumor and hearsay, making no real attempts to ascertain the truth concerning the management of the Indians in the Fort Bridger area.

Green River Ferry—1852

Another difficulty between the territorial officials and the residents of the Fort Bridger region developed over the control of the ferry rights on the Green River. The legislature of the State of Deseret had granted the first ferry rights on the Green River on 12 February 1850. Later, the Utah territorial legislature, in an act approved 16 January 1852, granted these ferry rights to one Thomas Moor for one year. The act also provided that if any person should erect "any public ferry across said river within Utah Territory, without permission of the legislature of Utah, said person or persons shall pay the sum of one thousand dollars, to be collected for the use of Utah."[12]

The passage of this ordinance giving the territory full right to control the ferries on the Green River caused much excitement among the whites and Indians in the area. For several years previous, the mountain men had operated ferries for the accommodation of travelers, and now the Mormons were

GREEN RIVER FERRY SITES

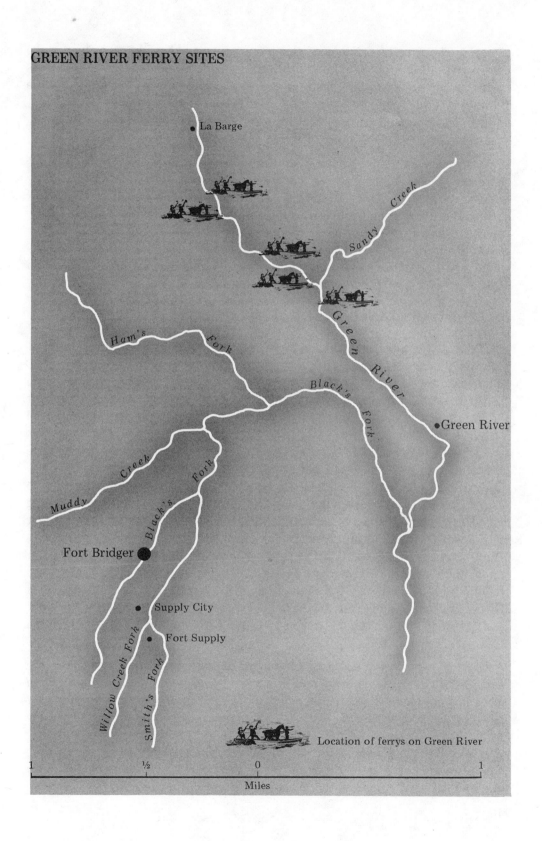

La Barge

Sandy Creek

Green River

Ham's Fork

Black's fork

Green River

Muddy Creek

Black's Fork

Fort Bridger

Black's Fork

Supply City

Fort Supply

Willow Creek Fork

Smith's Fork

Location of ferrys on Green River

1   ½   0   1

Miles

ignoring the squatters' rights of the mountain men. Unable to influence the territorial legislature, the mountain men took advantage of their close relations with the Shoshones to stir them up against the Mormons by claiming that the Mormons were driving the Indians off their lands.

In a letter written from Fort Bridger on 9 October 1852 to Agent Holeman, a citizen described the feelings of the Indians:

I beg to call your attention to the disturbed state of the Snake Indians at this moment in consequence of the occupation of a part of their country by the Mormon Whites. Being an American citizen and having the welfare and honor of my country in view I believe it is imperative for you, without delay, to allay, by all means in your authority, the present excitement. I saw the chiefs here [Fort Bridger], in council, at this fort, and heard them assert, that they intended to immediately drive the whites from their lands, and much persuasion was used to pacify them for the present time. And now, dear sir, if you do not use the authority vested in you, speadily, I do believe and fear scenes of destruction and bloodshed will soon ensue.[13]

Holeman, commenting on this letter, stated that he visited this section of country immediately and found a company of Mormons, under the charter of the legislature of Utah Territory, assembling on Green River to commence the construction of a bridge. However, they found so much opposition on the part of the Indians that they abandoned construction for the present and returned to Salt Lake City.

There was indeed at that time a group of Mormons on Green River. Since Brigham Young had received permission from the Shoshones to colonize the Green River area, he had addressed a letter to the Church members who were emigrating to Utah concerning his wishes to make a settlement there. Young asked for volunteers to remain on the Green River and establish a permanent settlement for the Mormons in that region. The letter, carried by Dimick B. Huntington, brought results, for a small group did remain on the Green River under the direction of Huntington with the intentions of erecting bridges and building a small settlement. This was the group Holeman found on the Green River. Brigham Young, realizing that the trouble Holeman referred to was very real, wrote to Huntington and others at Green River and recalled them with the following instructions:

I wrote to you on the 4th inst. per Indian Simons, to return from that place and for all you to come away and bring your effects with you to this city and leave not one behind. . . . It is needless to urge the matter of settlement at that place at the present. We do not wish to lay the foundation for any difficulty which by a little foresight may be avoided. . . .

If some of our people would go out with the Indians upon their trip hunting and get acquainted with them and with their chiefs, then a good influence might be exerted among them, which would not be in the power of anybody else to counteract, but we must wait for the present, therefore, all of you come back and let things take their course a little longer.[14]

Taxation

Another problem that existed between the mountain men in the Fort Bridger area and the Mormon leaders was the tax placed on the mountain men by the territorial legislature. Holeman summed up the problem as follows:

The Mormon authorities have levied a tax on these Mountaineers and have collected in some instances—as the tax is considered extravagant, and partly for the use and benefit of the Mormon Church, it is producing much excitement, and I fear will produce bloodshed. These men declare their willingness to pay any tax which the Government may demand, but refuse to pay a Mormon Tax as they term it.[15]

Although the tax was being levied not by the Mormon Church but by the territory of Utah, it was very difficult to separate the two, if one were a "gentile." Actually there was very little separation of state and church at this time among the Mormon people, and so the mountaineers had a point.

Legality of Liquor at Fort Bridger

The sale of liquor at Fort Bridger also became one of the sore points between the Mormons and Jim Bridger. An 1853 raid on the fort by the Mormons to arrest Bridger for illegal traffic with the Indians revealed a considerable supply of liquor at the fort. It is important to note that the sale and use of liquor at the fort was perfectly legal until the beginning of the Walker War in 1853 when Governor Young revoked all licenses to trade with the Indians. Holeman writing on 3 November 1852 said:

I wish, also, advise in relationship to use of spirituous liquors. On route from the states to Salt Lake City, there are two establishments for the accommodation of travelers, and emigration. I have given them licenses, as Indian traders, being in the Indian Country—they keep spirits for the use of the traveler, but in no case, do they permit the use of it by the Indians. They are what may be termed Tavern Keepers.[16]

Holeman had reference to the Green River crossing where the trappers had a tavern and Fort Bridger where Bridger and Vasquez had a tavern permit.

At the close of 1852, the feelings between the Mormon leaders and the mountaineers, particularly Bridger, were growing critical. The coming of the Mormons had taken away the majority of the fort's trade. The Mormons could now control the ferries on the Green River by due process of law under the Utah territorial legislature, and, to make matters worse, taxes were being levied. All these items plus the Mormon desire to control the Fort Bridger-Green River area, which was the eastern entrance into the Salt Lake Valley, led to a major showdown in 1853.

5

In the '70s, western artist W. H. Jackson painted the early fort from memory.

Mormons raid Fort Bridger

Difficulties between Jim Bridger and Brigham Young reached a climax in the late summer of 1853 when the Mormon leader became convinced that the mountain man was engaging in illegal trade with the Indians as well as stirring up enmity between the natives and the Mormons. The so-called "Walker War" in the summer of 1853 had caused the Mormon leader to rescind all licenses to trade with the Indians in any part of the territory, and, of course, this included Fort Bridger.

Part of the difficulty developed when the territorial legislature granted Mormon Church leader Daniel H. Wells a charter to operate the Green River ferries from 1853 to 1856. Wells transferred this right to Captain W. J. Hawley, but he and his partners were driven away by the mountaineers. Bill Hickman, who was selling merchandise in the region, explained the problem. He does not mention the charter transfer from Wells to Hawley, but otherwise he describes the situation accurately:

*During the summer a difficulty took place between the ferrymen and moun-
tainmen. The latter had always owned and run the ferry across Green River;
but the Utah Legislature granted a charter to Hawley, Thompson, and
McDonald, for all the ferries there. The Mountain Men, who had lived there for
many years, claimed their rights to be the oldest, and a difficulty took place, in
which the mountain men took forcible possession of all the ferries but one,
making some thirty thousand dollars out of them. When the ferrying season*

was over, the party having the charter brought suit against them for all they had made during the summer.[1]

The ferrymen were unsuccessful in collecting any damages.

When Hickman and other Mormon ferry operators returned to Salt Lake City and described the lawless situation at the ferries and the activities of Bridger, Governor Young ordered Sheriff James Ferguson to organize a posse, and proceed to Fort Bridger. Ferguson was instructed to seize any illegal goods, arrest Jim Bridger, and bring him to Salt Lake City for trial. Young's order was based on the following warrant issued by Associate Supreme Court Justice Shaver:

United States of America
Territory of Utah
Great Salt Lake County

To Joseph S. Heywood United States Marshal, or to any Sheriff or Constable of said Territory, Greeting:

Whereas information and complaint upon oath hath this day been made before me, Leonidas Shaver. Associate Justice of the Supreme Court of the United States for the Territory of Utah, charging that one James Bridger of said Territory has on the 1st day of 1853 unlawfully aided and abetted the Utah Indians, and supplyed them with arms and ammunition for the purpose of committing depredation upon and making war on the citizens of United States in said Territory—These are therefore to command you forthwith to arrest the said James Bridger and bring him before me or some Justice of the Peace in Great Salt Lake City, to answer the charges aforesaid, and, further to be dealt with according to Law—And for so doing this shall be your sufficient authority.

Given under my hand the 17th day of Aug 1853.

Leonidas Shaver [2]

Isaac C. Haight, a prominent Mormon, reported meeting the posse en route and gave his version of its purpose:

. . . We met a large posse going out to arrest Bridger and some of his gang that resisted the authorities of Utah. They have stirred up the Indians to commit depredations upon our people and some of our people have been killed, among others brother Dixon, that lived with Elder Taylor.[3]

50

Official document of the roughly drafted warrant issued to Bridger by Shaver.

William Hickman, Mormon sheriff.   Sheriff James Ferguson, posse leader.

When the posse of one hundred and fifty men arrived at the fort, they could not find Bridger, even after several days of searching. His Indian wife claimed she did not know where he had gone. There appears to have been little doubt that Bridger was guilty of disregarding the decree from Governor Young concerning the selling of lead and powder to the Indians. Fear of the Mormons apparently induced him to go into hiding in anticipation of arrest.

After carrying out the orders regarding the Fort Bridger property, some of the posse went on the Green River where they engaged in a battle with the mountaineers at the ferries. The posse killed two or three mountain men and took much of their property, including whiskey and several hundred head of livestock. Hickman commented that the members of the posse destroyed the "good stock of whiskey and rum in small doses."

When the sheriff and his assistants returned to Salt Lake City with the livestock, they reported authoritatively that the Mormons were now in Green River Valley to stay, and that Bridger was either gone for good or, if he returned, his influence would be minimized.

Bridger's mysterious departure and whereabouts remained a mystery for some time. The following statement written by Mary Ellie Smith, a resident of Salt Lake City in 1853, is indicative of the type of rumors that arose concerning the Mormon treatment of Bridger:

52

Orson Hyde, Green River Colonizer.   *Isaac Bullock colonized Fort Supply.*

*I knew many of the men who were members of this party, and **I** heard James Ferguson, Hiram Norton, Wiley Norton and Andrew Cunningham and many others, relate all they were at liberty to tell of it after they returned. The party, with Andrew Cunningham in command, arrived at the fort and found Bridger gone. But his wife was there living quietly as usual. She knew nothing of her husband. Cunningham judged rightly, as it afterwards proved, that Bridger was concealed in the mountains not far off and that he must either return occasionally to the fort for food or that those at the fort must communicate with him for this purpose. He therefore withdrew his party, professedly with a view of giving up the enterprise and returning to the city, but afterwards came back with a number of his men and stationed them in secure positions from which strict watch could be kept upon the movements of the fort. The measure was well taken; but Bridger was not easily decoyed, and it took an experienced ranger of the mountains to mislead him or to conceal the signs of what was passing from his practiced eye. It proved therefore to be a long siege. Many weeks passed and no trace of Bridger was found; but the faith of the Mormon leader was strong and he was content to abide his time, and he redoubled his watchfulness.*

The wife was at last detected in holding communication with the proscribed man, no sign of whose whereabouts had before been discovered. What was his

53

James S. Brown, Mormon missionary.   *George A. Smith, Mormon colonizer.*

fate, or that of his family none but the few Danites who were engaged in that mission can tell; and for some reason, the same men who had spoken freely to me of other crimes, were silent upon this point. When asked what became of him they did not know. A large amount of property was taken from the fort to the city, among which were arms, powder and lead.[4]

Dr. Thomas Flint, who arrived at Fort Bridger on August 27, recorded the following concerning the takeover of Fort Bridger by the territorial office:

. . . [I] went to the fort for ammunition but found the fort in possession of the territorial officer. Mormons . . . had 24 hours before driven old man Bridger out and taken possession. . . . Here Bridger had established his trading post many years before his fort had been taken by the Mormons with a good supply of merchandise selected for the Indian trade.[5]

More explicit information was recorded in a diary by a Mormon, John Brown, who was en route to Salt Lake Valley:

At Fort Bridger I found Capt. James Cummings with twenty men in possession of the fort he had come out here in the summer to arrest Mr. Bridger for

54

treason. Affidavids having been made to the effect that he had sold or furnished hostile Indians with ammunitions and etc. He made his escape but some of the posse were still here. They left for home however when we passed we being the last emigrants of the season.[6]

It would appear that part of the Mormon posse, at least twenty out of one hundred and fifty, remained at the fort from August 27 until October 7 looking for Bridger. This seizure and occupation of Bridger's establishment was distorted by later writers, and Bridger himself added to the misinformation and misunderstanding. For example, Captain R. B. Marcy, a close friend of Bridger's, recorded the mountaineer's own version of the event in his *Thirty Years of Army Life*, published in 1874:

Here he erected an establishment which he called Fort Bridger and here he was for several years prosecuting a profitable traffic both with the Indians and with California emigrants. At length, however, his prosperity excited the cupidity of the Mormons, and they intimated to him that his presence in such close proximity to their settlements was not agreeable, and advised him to pull up stakes and leave forthwith; and upon his questioning the legality or justice of this arbitrary summons, they came to his place with a force of avenging angels and forced him to make his escape to the woods in order to save his life. Here he remained secreted for several days, and through the assistance of his Indian wife, was enabled to elude the search of the Danites and make his way to Fort Laramie, leaving all his cattle and other property in possession of the Mormons.[7]

In 1873, twenty years after the raid, Bridger dictated a letter to Massachusetts Senator Benjamin F. Butler soliciting his political aid in connection with claims for compensation, and gave the following exaggerated account:

I was robbed and threatened with death by the Mormons, by the direction of Brigham Young, of all of my merchandise, livestock, in fact everything I possessed, amounting to more than $100,000 worth, the building in the fort partially destroyed by fire, and I barely escaped with my life.[8]

There is no evidence that Bridger was threatened with death, but only with arrest, and the fort was not partially destroyed by fire as Bridger testified in writing to Senator Butler. Bridger was guilty of trying to use the burning of the fort in 1857 by the Mormons to dramatize his losses in the 1853 raid.

Actually, the sheriff and posse kept itemized ledgers from the time of their arrival in August 1853 until their departure in October, keeping careful track of each item that was purchased from the fort's commissary or used while the posse resided at the fort. The ledgers are available and show that $802.91

worth of merchandise was either purchased or used during that period. Also, ledgers on all items taken from the fort back to Salt Lake City are available and reveal that a total of $1,433.30 worth of merchandise representing knives, caps, lead balls, powder, iron, guns—both pistols and rifles—was taken. They also show that $500.00 was entered for rent for the "occupation of fort and houses near 2 months." Thus a total of $2,736.21 was the acknowledged debt owed to Bridger by the territorial government. The following statement found with the invoice turned over to Mormon leaders on the return of the posse from Fort Bridger is interesting. "The above goods are charged at the established prices of the county given under my hand this the 25th day of February, 1854. James Bridger."

This item on the ledger was not signed by Bridger since he could not write, nor was it written by his consent since he had gone east and could not be found. If Vasquez were available to approve the fixed price, he would have signed for both himself and Bridger as he did on all other documents. Therefore, it would appear that Bridger's name was entered on the ledgers to finalize them and to close the books since neither Bridger nor Vasquez was available at the time.

In 1858, when the final payment was made to Bridger and Vasquez for the fort, a settlement was also made concerning the merchandise taken and used at the fort in 1853. It appears that Bridger and Vasquez did not feel that the purchase price of $8,000 completely covered the loss of $2,763.21 sustained by them in 1853, so a separate payment of $1,000 was paid to Bridger and Vasquez on 18 October 1858.

The following is the receipt signed by Vasquez for himself and Bridger upon payment of the $1,000:

Received Great Salt Lake City, Utah Territory, October eighteenth, one thousand eight hundred and fifty eight of Lewis Robison the sum of one thousand dollars, lawful money of the United States in full payment according to mutual agreement, for all and severally the goods, cattle, house rent etc. etc., taken and used by said Lewis Robison, James Ferguson, James W. Cummings and others (including guns, lead balls, powder, knives etc. taken by order of Governor Brigham Young, ex officio superintendent of Indian Affairs of Utah Territory as contraband trade) at Fort Bridger in the year one thousand eight hundred and fifty three.

Witnesses   *Louis Vasquez*
John Hartnell   *for*
James Ferguson   *Bridger and Vasquez*[9]

From the ledger, it is apparent that Bridger's holdings at the fort which were used or taken by the posse amounted to almost $3,000. That the value of the

Property Belonging to Bridger and Vasques Taken forcible possession of By the authorities of Utah Territory, from 25th of August, to 1st of September 1853.

Louis Robison's receipt for Quartermaster and Commissary Stores; as Commissary and Quarter Master of Utah Territory. $266.16

J. W. Cummins, Receipt as Capt Commanding Fort Bridger Expedition 536.75

James Fergusons Receipts as Commander of Fort Bridger & Greenriver Expedition, for Guns (and what he stiles Central and Indian trade) Powder Ball Caps, & Knives.

39½ Doz Best quality Knives assorted 9.00 a vy	355.50
17600 Caps. 3.00 a thousand	52.80
25 N. W. Guns at 15.00 each	375.00
200 lbs lead Balls 50 cts per lb.	100.00
100 lbs powder 1.50 per lb	150.00
12 Rifle Guns; some of them out of Repair $25.00	300.00
" 1 Black Smiths Anville	50.00
Iron and Steal used in Blacksmithing	50.00
Occupation of Fort and Houses near 2 months	500.00
	$2736.21

The above goods are Charged at the established prices of the Country given under my hand this the 23rd day of February 1854   James Bridger

Bridger Ranch 1853.
Invoice and Receipts of property received of Jos Bridger.

Accounts & Receipts

The invading posse kept this ledger of what they used at the Fort. (See p. 175.)

*Received Great Salt Lake City, Utah
Territory, October eighteenth, one thousand eight
hundred and fifty eight of Lewis Robison the
sum of One Thousand Dollars, lawful money
of the United States in full payment according to mutual agreement, for all and severally
the goods, Cattle, house-rent &c &c taken and
used by said Lewis Robison, James Ferguson
James W. Cummings and others (including Guns
Lead Balls, Powder, Knives &c taken by order of
Governor Brigham Young, ex-officio Superintendent
of Indian affairs of Utah Territory as contraband Indian trade) at Fort Bridger in the year
One thousand eight hundred and fifty three.*

Witnesses

John Hartnell

James Ferguson

Louis Vasquez

Bridger & Vasquez

Bridger Ranch.   Oct 18th 1858

$1000   Cash Receipt

In full for Bridger Ranch.

Bridger & Vasquez

Mormon leaders paid a $1,000 settlement for the 1853 occupancy of the fort.

58

remaining merchandise and the fort itself was worth several thousand more cannot be questioned. But the sum of $100,000 claimed by Bridger to be the value placed on the fort in 1853 when he escaped arrest by the Mormon posse included a goodly sum of "heart balm."

The old mountain man must have remained in Green River Valley, for soon after the posse left on 17 October 1853, Bridger and John M. Hockaday, a government surveyor, began a land survey of the area claimed by Bridger. On 6 November 1853 the survey was completed, revealing that the plat contained 3,898 acres and two rods. The following spring, 16 March 1854, a copy was filed with Thomas Bullock, Great Salt Lake County Recorder, and with the General Land Office in Washington, D.C., on 9 March 1854.

Prior to this Bridger had another deed recorded on some property he had purchased from Charles Sagenes on 28 August 1852. This property was near Fort Bridger and consisted of five houses with some acreage. Bridger paid Sagenes four hundred dollars for his property, which was later included in the survey by John M. Hockaday. This bill of sale was recorded at the Great Salt Lake County offices on 28 October 1853.

After completing the survey of Fort Bridger, the mountaineer took his family and settled on a farm at Little Santa Fe, Jackson County, Missouri, near Kansas City. Even though Bridger had left Fort Bridger, he was still a thorn in the side of the Mormon leaders. Brigham Young, in a dictated letter addressed to Stephen A. Douglas in April 1854, expressed concern because Bridger:

... had become the oracle in Congress, in all matters pertaining to Utah; that he had informed Congress that Utah had dared to assess and collect taxes; that the Mormons must have killed Capt. Gunnison, because the Pauvenetes had not guns ... that the Mormons were an outrageous set, with no redeeming qualities. Gov. Young expressed his astonishment that Bridger should be sought after for information on any point when a gentlemen like Delegate Bernhisel was accessible.[10]

Mormons Colonize Green River County

In October 1853, the Mormon leaders thought they were now in a position to establish a permanent colony in Green River Valley, and thus gain control of that portion of the territory. Orson Hyde was called to organize the colony, and on the last day of the General Conference in October 1853, the Mormon Apostle read the names of thirty-nine persons who had been called by the Church leaders to serve in the "Green River Mission."

On November 1 this company gathered at the Council House in Salt Lake City and were organized under the direction of Captain John Nebeker, who led them on their eleven-day march to the famous fort.

As soon as the first company was on its way toward the settlement, Orson Hyde busied himself in raising another company to follow the first. In less than two weeks, a group consisting of fifty-three men, primarily volunteers, had been raised and fitted with supplies and necessary tools and implements. With Isaac Bullock as captain, this group left Salt Lake City three days after the first company had arrived at Fort Bridger.

When the first company of Mormon colonists arrived at Fort Bridger, they found about a dozen angry mountaineers living there. Having had two or three of their number killed at the Green River ferry by the Mormon posse only a few weeks earlier, they were antagonistic to any Mormon plan to occupy the fort until a site for a permanent settlement could be chosen. According to James Brown, the Mormons were "considerably cowed" by the "twelve or fifteen rough mountain men" who seemed to be "very surly and suspicious," while the "spirit of murder and death appeared to be lurking in their minds."[11] Consequently, the colonizers, unprepared for such a reception, soon lost interest in occupying the post. They learned that about twenty additional mountain men, together with a tribe of Ute Indians, were in the area. It appeared to the Mormons that the valley was "held in the fists of a well organized band of from seventy-five to a hundred desperadoes" and so the fearful group moved on to Smith's Fork, where they camped while a committee selected a suitable place for a settlement. They located a site about two miles above the confluence of Willow Creek and Smith's Fork at a point approximately twelve miles from Fort Bridger. Nebeker's party was joined on Smith's Fork by the second group sent out from Salt Lake City, and together they established a settlement known as Fort Supply. In speaking of the arrival of the second group, one of the original members, James S. Brown, remarked that "on November 26th, 1853, Captain Isaac Bullock came in with fifty-three men and twenty-five wagons. When they joined us our company was ninety-two strong, all well armed and when our block house was completed we felt safer than ever."[12]

By the end of 1853, Orson Hyde had fulfilled his assignment of starting a settlement in Green River Valley, but apparently was not happy with the prospects. In the spring of 1854, when Hyde was traveling east and stopped at Fort Supply, Hosea Stout, one of Hyde's traveling companions, gave his opinion of the new settlement when he wrote:

It is the most forbidding and godforsaken place I have ever seen for an attempt to be made for a settlement and judging from the altitude I have no hesitancy in predicting that it will yet prove a total failure but the Brethren here have done a great deal of labor. . . . Elder Hyde seems to have an invincible repugnance to Fort Supply.[13]

However, the benefits derived from this outpost justified the project in the eyes of the Church leaders, who made plans to establish Fort Supply as a permanent settlement. It became a resting place for the emigrating Saints, a

60

Fort Supply, settlement built by the Mormons in Green River County, 1853-57.

place to replenish their food supplies, an Indian mission and a defense against the mountain men's activities among the Indians. If it had been permitted to continue, Fort Supply would very probably be a community in Uinta County, Wyoming, today, whereas at the present time there is nothing left of the establishment except stumps in the ground—remnants of what the Mormon settlers built there in 1853-57.

It did serve as a Mormon center in Green River Valley, and a companion colony to Fort Bridger after this post was purchased and occupied by the Mormons in 1855.

61

6

Mormon leader Lewis Robison built this cobblestone wall at the fort in 1857.

Mormons purchase and expand Fort Bridger

Although the Mormons had built Fort Supply instead of occupying Fort Bridger, they continued to show an interest in acquiring the older post. It actually came under the political jurisdiction of the Mormons in the winter of 1853-54, when Green River County was organized as a part of Utah Territory. The official announcement read:

Whereas the Boundaries of Green River County in the territory of Utah were defined and attached to Great Salt Lake County for election, revenue, and Judicial purposes by a special act of the legislature of said Territory approved March the 3rd 1852, and was detached from said Great Salt Lake County by another act of said legislature approved January 13th 1854, and is now organized with its Judiciary and officers and lies in the first Judicial District of the United States Court for said Territory.[1]

In addition to Fort Supply and Fort Bridger, the county included the ferries on the Green River. W. I. Appleby was appointed probate judge, Robert Alexander, clerk of probate court, and William A. Hickman, county sheriff. Hickman was also made prosecuting attorney, assessor, and tax collector, and assigned by Brigham Young to use his influence in quieting down the mountaineers in that section of the country. The county seat was established at the Mormon ferries, but it was difficult to have a government agency there because of the continuing difficulties with the mountaineers and the Indians. Clearly Fort Bridger would be a more suitable center for county government.

Daniel H. Wells, Mormon general.   *Lewis Robison succeeded Bridger.*

Renewed Conflict over the Green River Ferry Rights

As mentioned previously, Daniel H. Wells was granted a charter on 17 January 1853 to erect ferries for the conveyance of stock wagons, passengers, etc., over the Green River. The charter required Wells to pay into the treasury of the Perpetual Emigrating Fund Company ten per cent of all proceeds. The right to the Green River ferries was granted to him for three years beginning 15 May 1853. Wells was expected to maintain ferries at two of the most convenient and safe places of crossing on the Sublette Cutoff and on the Salt Lake Road.

This charter was transferred by Wells to Captain W. J. Hawley, James H. Jones, John Kerr, Frances M. Russell, and John M. Russell in the spring of 1854. Subsequently, by an act of the Utah Legislature approved 27 December 1855, Isaac Bullock and Lewis Robison were granted the exclusive right and privilege of ferries across Green River for the space of three years from 15 May 1856, succeeding Daniel H. Wells as the statutory owners of the Green River ferry rights. Alfred Cumming, who succeeded Brigham Young as governor of Utah Territory in 1858, was against the granting of special privileges in the shape of herdgrounds, ferries, etc., and in 1859 all such special grants were repealed.

Questions concerning the Mormon policies regarding Indian rights in regard to the ferries were raised by John M. Hockaday who on 17 June 1854 wrote to

64

George W. Manypenny, commissioner of Indian affairs, expressing the Indians' dissatisfaction with the Mormon policies and supporting the rights of the mountain men to the ferries because of their marriages with Indian women, and the legal rights of the Indians to the land. He wrote

that there has been no treaty made with the Indians and that the land, timber, rivers etc. legally belong to them, until purchased of them by treaty with the United States Government, and that the Legislature of the Territory of Utah have no right or authority to grant such Charters on Indian lands. . .[2]

Second Lieutenant H. B. Fleming of Fort Laramie, in a letter to the Commissioner, explained the situation more clearly.

Sir

A copy of a letter has been sent me requesting me to forward the same to you for your decision thereon. There has been a great deal of trouble between the Mountain Men and the Mormons for some time past, which has resulted in the death of several persons on both sides. The Mountain Men have wives and children among the Snake Indians, and therefore claim the right to the Green River country in virtue of the grant given them by the Indians to whom the country belongs; as no treaty has yet been made to extinguish their title—The Mormons on the other hand claim jurisdiction over the country, paramount to all Indian titles in virtue of it being in Utah Territory.

Now, the question, in issue appears to me this; since the country lies in the Territory of Utah, have the Mormons or have they not the right to dispose of the country to settlers, to dispose of its resources, revenues, and finally everything in the country or exercise judicial power over revenues before the actual Indian Title has been extinguished.

These questions have been and are now agitated among the people of the new Territories—have caused a great deal of trouble and will cause more unless permanently settled by a proper authority. . . . Your decision in this case I consider of great importance as it is time such things were settled and unnecessary blood-shed saved by placing the right where it properly belongs. Both parties contend for the right and I might add both equally honest in their convictions.[3]

Since there was no federal treaty with the Shoshone pertaining to the Green River lands, the commissioner was unable to help the Indians. The law was in the hands of the territorial legislature and its enforcement in the territorial courts. The Mormons, who controlled both the courts and the legislature had all the legal rights needed to maintain the ferries on the Green River.

The problem of the Green River ferries was a continuous battle and was never really brought to a conclusion for several years, although there was no question that the Mormons had gained the upper hand after the spring of 1854.

Mormons Purchase Fort Bridger

Despite the unfriendly relationship that had developed between Jim Bridger and the Mormons, the old mountaineer recognized them as the best prospective buyers of his outpost, and finally decided to accept the offer the agents of the Mormon Church made to him. Since there has been considerable controversy concerning the time and details of this purchase, it is appropriate to examine the results of extensive research on the problem. Accounts have varied all the way from Bridger's claim that he was "run off" of his property without ever receiving payment, to Mormon Church Historian Andrew Jenson's assertion that prior to November 1853 Brigham Young had "purchased of James Bridger a Mexican Grant for thirty square miles of land and some cabins afterwards known as Fort Bridger. This was the first property owned by the Church in Green River Country."[4]

A letter written by Lewis Robison, the Mormon purchasing agent, to Daniel H. Wells, dated 5 August 1855, found recently in the LDS Church Historical Department appears to answer some of the questions concerning the possession of Fort Bridger from the time of Bridger's escape until the purchase of the fort in August 1855. This letter reports that the mountain men controlled Fort Bridger until the spring of 1855 when Bridger returned and resided there until he sold it to Lewis Robison on 3 August 1855. The Mormons did not take possession of the fort until it had been legally purchased. This document, which is now available to scholars, is important in clearing up the controversy of the purchase of the fort by the Mormons, and should put an end to misunderstandings and false accusations against the Mormon Church.

According to this research, when Bridger escaped arrest by the posse in August 1853, he returned to the east, spending much time in Washington, D.C., trying to legalize his title to the property and seeking redress through the federal government for the losses he had sustained at the hands of the Mormons. Unsuccessful in his efforts, Bridger returned to the mountains in the spring of 1855. John L. Smith reported on 19 June 1855 that "near Fort Kearney I met Bridger on his way to the mountains." During the summer of 1855 William A. Hickman, an agent of the Mormon Church, approached Bridger about selling his fort. Lewis Robison arrived at Fort Supply on Tuesday, 31 July 1855, to make the final transaction. William A. Hickman had been in contact with Bridger prior to July 31, waiting for Bridger to make up his mind if he would sell. Hickman arrived at Fort Supply on Wednesday, August 1, and told Robison that the mountain men were putting pressure on Bridger not to sell and that Bridger seemed to be still "careless and indifferent." Robison went to Fort Bridger on Thursday, August 2, and found that Bridger would not reduce the $8,000 price he had earlier indicated would be his selling price. Vasquez was not present at this time, but knowing of the plans to sell, had commissioned H. F. Morrell to be his agent. Robison, realizing that Bridger would not reduce his selling price, told Bridger that he would take him

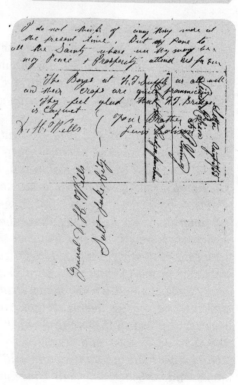

This important letter, found by the authors, is transcribed in the appendix.

The sole remnant of Mormon improvements on the fort is a section of the wall.

at his offer of $4,000 and pay the balance in fifteen months. Bridger then started to hedge when he realized that Robison was willing to pay the price, and pointed out that he felt he should get $600 to $800 more. When Robison told him he would not give him a dime more, Bridger finally agreed to sell. Robison had prepared the following agreement which he asked Bridger to sign:

I, James Bridger of the firm of Bridger and Vasquez of Green River County Utah Territory for and in consideration of the sum of   thousand dollars to me in hand paid by Lewis Robison of Great Salt Lake County in said Territory. Do hereby sell, transfer, set over, convey, and confirm, unto the said Lewis Robison his heirs or assigns. All of my rights, title, claim possession or estated personal and real belonging unto the firm known as Bridger and Vasquez or either of us now lying and being in said Territory and Green River County. A fore said consisting principally of cattle, horses, goods, flour, sundry articles of personal property and the entire claim, Stand, Trading post, herding ground and Lands claimed by me James Bridger and Louis Vasquez, together with all our interest prospective as well as present and give and confirm the great and peaceable possession there of from this time forward firmly binding myself also the firm of Bridger and Vasquez to use due deligence and the utmost of our ability to obtain a Grant of the said Premises from the United States government and also agreeing and covenanting that we will make conveyance and good warrantee deed and title to the same when obtained from said Govern-

68

I James Bridger of the firm of Bridger and Vasquez of Green River County Utah Territory for and in consideration of the sum of _____ thousand Dollars to me in hand paid by Lewis Robison of Great Salt Lake County in said Territory Do hereby Sell, transfer set over, convey and confirm, unto the said Lewis Robison his heirs or assigns, All of my right, title, claim possession or Estate personal and Real belonging unto the firm known as Bridger and Vasquez or either of us now lying and being in said Territory and Green River County Aforesaid consisting principally of Cattle, horses, goods, flour sundry articles of personal property and The Entire Claim, Stand Trading Post, herding ground and Lands claimed by me James Bridger and Louis Vasquez, together with all our interest prospective as well as present and give and confirm the quiet and peaceable possession thereof from this time forward firmly binding myself as also the firm of Bridger and Vasquez to use due diligence and the utmost of our ability to obtain a Grant of the said Premises from the United States government and also agreeing and covenanting that we will make conveyance and good Warrantee deed and title to the same when obtained from said Government unto the said Lewis Robison his heirs or assigns without further cost, expense or consideration on the part of Said Robison — To all of which we bind ourselves individually and collectively our heirs and assigns executors or administrators firmly by these presents in the sum of Eight thousand dollars for the faithful full and complete fulfillment of this agreement and for a failure on our part to pay or cause to be paid unto the said Robison his heirs or assigns the above specified amount without fail or defalcation

Signed Sealed and delivered at Fort Bridger in said County of Green river and Territory of Utah this _____ day of _____ 1855.

Bridger turned down this contract Robison offered him to purchase the fort.

ment unto the said Lewis Robison his heirs or assigns with out further cost expenses or consideration on the part of said Robison to all of which we bind ourselves individually and collectively our heirs and assigns executors or administrators firmly by these present in the sum of Eight thousand dollars for the faithful full and complete fulfillment of this agreement and for a failure on our part to pay or cause to be paid unto the said Robison his heirs or assigns the above specified amount without fail or defalcification.

Signed sealed and delivered at Fort Bridger in said county of Green River Territory of Utah this   Day of 1855[5]

However, Bridger refused to accept this agreement because he did not have a legal title to the property and refused to obtain a title "more than he now had which was only possession."

Bridger claimed that he had a "first rate lawyer" boarding with him that could "do business upright," but did not identify him. It seems likely that this lawyer was H. F. Morrell, the agent of Vasquez, who signed the following acceptable contract for Bridger's portion on 3 August 1855:

August 3, 1855

Fort Bridger Utah Territory Green River Co.

This indenture made and entered into this day and date where written witnesses that Bridger and Vasquez of the first part for and in consideration of the sum of Eight Thousand Dollars, one half in hand Paid and the other half to be paid in fifteen months from this day here this day bargained sold and conveyed and by these present do bargain sell and convey to Lewis Robison of the second part all the right title and interest both real and personal to which we have say claim in said Green River County Utah Territory consisting of the following property to wit—Twenty miles square of land more or less upon which is situated the hereditaments and the Buildings known as Fort Bridger Buildings consisting of the ranch and herd ground together with all the right title and interest of the said party of the first part to all and every article of property belonging to said post including cattle, horses, goods, groceries, and etc. Now if the said party of the second part shall well and truly pay to the said party of the first part the sum of Four Thousand Dollars in fifteen months from this date, then this bond to be in full force and effect in law, otherwise to be null and void and the property above described to revert back to the said party of the first part. In witness whereof we have here unto set our hands and seals this day and date above written in presence

Almirin Grow
Wm. A. Hickman

70

Jas X Bridger
Louis Vasquez
per H. F. Morrell agent[6]

Bridger and Vasquez kept the original document while Robison had a copy made to send back to the Mormon leaders. In 1858, Vasquez appeared before the clerk of the County of Great Salt Lake, S. A. Gilbert, approved of Morrell as his agent and identified his signature on the indenture. This appearance and testimony was also recorded at the county clerk's office on October 21, 1858.

Territory of Utah
County of Great Salt Lake

Personally appeared before me, Samuel A. Gilbert, Clerk of the United States Court for the Third Judicial District of Utah Territory, Louis Vasquez who being duly sworn says that Hiram F. Morrell was his lawfully appointed Agent, and as such was authorized to sign the indenture referred to in the indenture hereto attached and bearing this date, and that he, the deponent doth fully approve of the Acts and doings of the said Morrell in the above premise as if done by himself in his own proper person.

Deponent further says that he is duly authorized to act for and in behalf of James Bridger aforesaid, and for him to sign the preceding indenture.

Louis Vasquez[7]

In testimony whereof I have hereunto set my hand and seal of Court at Salt Lake City in the Territory and County above named, this eighteenth day of October one thousand eight hundred and fifty eight.

Samuel A. Gilbert, Clerk

Recorded, October 21, 1858

On 5 August 1855, the same day he wrote Daniel H. Wells, Lewis Robison stated that he had possession of the fort and all its stock except for five oxen and one wagon which were on the Green River in the care of James Bridger. In a letter written to Daniel H. Wells on 13 August 1855 Robison explained that he had sent for the oxen and wagon. Robison also sent an invoice to Wells itemizing in detail all that had been purchased at the fort. He stated in his letter that he thought the total sum of merchandise and stock would be close to $5,000. Robison did not miss his estimate by much. The invoice prepared and sent by Robison listed the value of all items purchased excluding the five oxen and wagon at $4,727.30.

Fort Bridger, Utah Terity Green River Co

This indenture made and entered into this day and date above written witnesseth That Bridger & Vasques of the first part for and in Consideration of the sum of Eight Thousand Dollars one half in hand Paid and the other half to be paid in fifteen months from this date have this day bargained Sold and Conveyed and by these presents do Bargain Sell and Convey to Lewis Robison of the Second Part All the Right title and interest both real and Personal to which we have any Claim in said Green River County Utah Teritory Consisting of the following Property to wit — Twenty miles square of land more or less upon which is situated the heredilaments and appurtenances the Buildings Known as Fort Bridge, Buildings Consisting of the Ranch and Hured Ground together with all the right Title and interest of the said Party of the first part to all and any article of Property belonging to said Post including Cattle Horses Goods Groceries &c —

Now if the said Party of the Second Part Shall well and truly pay to the said Party of the first Part the sum of Four Thousand Dollars in fifteen Months from this date then this Bond to be in full force and effect in law, otherwise to be null and void and the Property above described to revert back to the said Party of the first Part In witness whereof we have hereunto set our hands and seals this day and date above written

in presence of
Almirin Grimm
Wm A Hickman

(Jas. his mark Bridger (Seal)
(Lewis Vasquez (Seal)
(per H T Morrell agent

The above is an exact Copy of the Contract given to me by Bridger & Vasques
Lewis Robison

A Copy of
Agreement from
Bridger & Vasques
to Lewis Robison

Bridger's attorney drew up this contract which was approved by both parties.
72

Territory of Utah   }
County of Great Salt Lake } ss.

Personally appeared before me
Samuel A. Gilbert, Clerk of the United
States Court for the Third Judicial District of Utah
Territory, Louis Vasquez who being duly sworn
says That Hiram F. Morrell was his lawfully
appointed agent, and as such was authorized
to sign the indenture referred to in the indenture
hereto attached and bearing this date, and that
he the deponent doth fully approve of the Acts
and doings of the said Morrel in the above
premises as if done by himself in his own
proper person.

Deponent further says that he
is duly authorized to act for and in behalf
of James Bryer aforesaid, and for him to
sign the preceding indenture.

(Signed)   Louis Vasquez.

In Testimony whereof I have hereunto set my
hand and seal of Court at Great Salt Lake
City in the Territory and County above named,
this eighteenth day of October — one thousand
eight hundred and fifty eight

{L S}   Signed   Samuel A. Gilbert Clerk

With this document Vasquez verifies both previous contract and final payment.

73

In the letter written to Wells on August 5, Robison asked Wells to write as soon as possible in answer to several questions he had in regard to some of the merchandise and the disposition of certain items. He explained that Bridger had left on the fourth day after the purchase of the fort was made. He inserted another letter which he had written on August 3 pertaining to the payment of $4,000 to Bridger and Vasquez:[8]

Fort Bridger, August 3, 1855

I have this day paid Jas. Bridger four thousand dollars it being one half the purchase money for the Fort Bridger property and in the payment there is nine hundred and sixty dollars of a gold money marked twenty dollars United States Assay Office of Gold San Francisco California—now if there is a discount on said gold in banks I hereby agree to make it good to said Bridger upon right proof being made to the fact.

Lewis Robison

*Witness
Almirin Grow*

The discount mentioned in this letter on the value of the gold at the time of payment which Robison promised to make good (if there was a difference), was transacted in 1858 when the final payment of $4,000 was made. Louis Vasquez signed the following note for Bridger and himself.[9]

Salt Lake City   *Oct. 20th 1858*

Received Twenty Four Dollars in full payment of discount on the within mentioned gold.

*Louis Vasquez
for
Bridger and Vasquez*

Robison concluded his letter to Wells by saying that the "boys at Fort Supply were glad that Fort Bridger was in the hands of the Church."

The following statement of William A. Hickman made in 1857 is further evidence that the post was purchased in 1855:

The post was then, and had been for two years, owned by the Church, and in possession of Mr. Robison, who had charge of the same from the time of its purchase, I having been one of the carriers of the heavy load of gold it took to purchase said place with the livestock and goods thereon.[10]

74

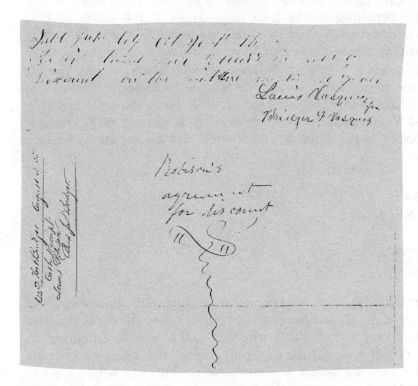

Fort Bridger Aug. 3" 1855.

I have this day Paid Ja. Bridger four thousand
dollars it being one half the Purchase money
for the Fort Bridger Property and in
the Payment there is nine hundred and
sixty dollars of Gold money marked twenty
dollars united States assay office of
Gold Sanfransisco California — now
if there is a discount on said
Gold in Banks I hereby agree to
make it Good to said Bridger
upon sight Proof being made of the fact

Witness   Lewis Robison

Almerin Grow

Lewis Robison verifies his payment of $4,000 to Jim Bridger for the fort.

This receipt verifies the payment to Louis Vasquez of gold-value difference.

The unfortunate thing about this quote is that historians and writers have been reluctant to put much faith in it since Hickman had gained a dubious reputation as a hired killer. However, it appears that Hickman was correct in his memory of the event.

Upon receiving the information from him on the purchase of the fort, Brigham Young wrote Robison on 9 August 1855, stating: "We are glad the purchase is made . . . the account is opened with Bridger Ranch."[11]

Mormon leader Heber C. Kimball writing to F. D. Richards in England stated: "The Church has bought out Bridger Ranch one hundred horned cattle, seven or eight horses, flour and goods and paid $8,000 for it, Bridger is gone."[12]

In a letter written to Lewis Robison from Daniel H. Wells dated 31 July 1856, it is apparent that the Church leaders were preparing to make the final payment, due by 3 November 1856, fifteen months from the day of purchase. "You will please forward to us the note in order to enable us to make the payment due this fall on the ranch. We must keep an eye out for that payment do you know where the note is?"[13] In answer to the Wells request concerning the note, Robison wrote: "The note we owe for the Ranch I presume is in the hands of Vasquez, tho I have no certain knowledge of it."[14]

In March 1856, seven months after the Mormons had purchased the fort, Bridger and Vasquez hired Timothy Goodale to be their lawful agent in handling the affairs pertaining to the final transactions of the selling of Fort Bridger. The location for the final payment was to be Salt Lake City. Why Goodale or, for that matter, Bridger or Vasquez, did not pick up the money is not known. In a letter written to Robison from Brigham Young, there is evidence that the money had been kept on reserve for Bridger or Vasquez or their agent to collect. Louis Vasquez had written Robison about the money in May 1856, and Vasquez's letter was forwarded to Brigham Young. Young in return told Robison to get in touch with Vasquez and get the matter straightened out.[15]

Presidents Office
GSL City 2nd June 1857

Bro. Lewis Robison
Bridger

Your note enclosing one from M. Vasquez is received. The money has been kept ready on hand for the last few years but now we have not got Bridger and Vasquez for us to pay it in St. Louis which we will be able to do during the summer there. Bro. Hor. S. Ellridge our agent there. If this arrangement would be agreeable to them we would like to know it. You had better write to Vasquez by this mail and ascertain the fact from his or Bridger, we have not a doubt but they would prefer it paid there, as it would save them the trouble and expense of sending for it, if they should accede to this arrangement, that is to accept of the payment in St. Louis from H. S. Ellridge, they can have it as soon as we can get the word and the mails can forward the necessary papers for the transaction of the business.

All is well with us here, God bless you and yours and the Faithful

Brigham Young

P.S. There ought to be a transfer, conveyance, or legal quit claim deed, conveying all right title etc. passed to us at or before the time of payment.

P.P. The address of M. Vasquez is Westport, Mo.

Young's letter seems to imply that it would be best for all concerned to have Bridger and Vasquez pick the money up in St. Louis from the Church agent there. However, it appears that the money was also made available in Salt Lake City if this should be convenient. From the events that transpired it appears that Bridger and Vasquez decided to pick up the money in Salt Lake City. Brigham Young writing to Robison in August 1857 stated: "We have made arrangements with Mr. Bell to settle with Bridger whenever he comes for his money."[16]

The final payment was not made until October 1858 when Vasquez arrived in Salt Lake City for the money. One of the reasons for the delay during the latter part of 1857 until the spring of 1858 was the difficulty involved with the approach of the federal army and Brigham Young's determination to resist it. Brigham Young's clerk made the following entry in Young's journal under the date of 16 October 1858: "Vasquez, the late partner of Jim Bridger, called upon Pre. Young this morning about the affairs at Fort Bridger."[17] Two days later the following entry was made:[18]

Louis Vasquez of the firm of Bridger and Vasquez executed a bill of sale of Fort Bridger and knowledge receipt of $4,000.00 on August 3, 1855 and $4,000.00 today also acknowledge before Samuel A. Gilbert, Clerk of the Third District Court, that Hiram F. Morrell was his lawfully appointed agent and that he approved of the acts and doings of said Morrell and in the sale of said property.

Thus on 18 October 1858, a year after the Mormons had burned Fort Bridger to the ground in face of the approaching army, the final payment of $4,000 was made in Salt Lake City to Louis Vasquez. The indenture which was signed by Vasquez was recorded at the county clerk's office in the city of Salt Lake. Vasquez testified before Samuel A. Gilbert, clerk of the county of Salt

Lake, that he was duly authorized to act on behalf of James Bridger. Also the indenture signed at Fort Bridger in 1855 at the first $4,000 payment was recorded in the county clerk's office on 21 October 1858.

Descriptions of Fort Bridger

Following this conclusive evidence of the legal purchase of the post by the Mormons, it may be interesting to examine what the fort looked like in 1855. In 1849 W. G. Johnston recorded one of the best descriptions of the fort available, mentioning the mountains looming up "grandly above the beautiful fertile valley," and the "log buildings surrounded by a high picket fence, and having a heavy wooden entrance gate." He and his companion visited several homes, one of which was the dwelling of Mrs. Vasquez who was so hospitable she invited them to "sit upon chairs, a situation some what novel" to which they were evidently unaccustomed. Johnston continues:

Opening upon a court were the rooms occupied by the Bridger family. Mr. Bridger, with a taste differing from that of his partner, who has a white wife from the states, made his selection from among the ladies of the wilderness, a stolid, fleshy, round-headed woman, not oppressed with the lines of beauty. Her hair was intensely black and straight and so cut that it hung in a thick mass upon her broad shoulders. . . .

He further describes the articles available at the fort, and the nature of his transactions with Bridger:

In a store room of the fort was a considerable stock of buffalo robes, one of which I purchased for the sum of five dollars. It was an exceedingly fine large robe with long silky hair, and its equal I have rarely seen. . . . Other store rooms were nearly bare of goods. In one was a keg of whiskey, a jar of tobacco, a box of clay pipes made of red stone called "st. Peter's Rock." said to have been brought from the upper Mississippi, and highly esteemed by Indians. The price at which they are sold to—five dollars each—would indicate that they are accounted valuable, while Mr. Bridger informed me that there is a very ready sale for them. . . . Our company, from a common fund, purchased a steer from Mr. Bridger, paying for it twenty dollars.[19]

Captain Howard Stansbury, in his report to the War Department concerning his explorations of the Great Salt Lake in 1849, gave a very good description of the fort. He was at the post from August 11 to August 20, during one of those rare times when Bridger was present. After making three river crossings, he came upon the fort,

. . . built in the usual form of pickets, which the lodging apartments and offices opening into a hollow square, protected from attack from without by a strong

78

gate of timber. On the north, and continuous with the walls, is a strong high picket fence, enclosing a large yard into which the animals belonging to the establishment are driven for protection from both wild beasts and Indians. We were received with great kindness and lavish hospitality by the proprietor, Major James Bridger. . . . Several of my wagons needed repair, the train was detained five days for the purpose, Major Bridger courteously placing his black-smith-shop at my service. [20]

On 15 July 1850, Madison Moorman recorded in his journal the following description of the condition of the fort and the nature of the Indians:

The fort is about a mile to the left of the road and is very much delapidated; being but little else than a trading post. A small number of men is posted here to keep the Indians in subjection—who belong to the Shoshonee or Snake tribe, and are very low, degraded and abandoned—living upon all kinds of insects, animals and reptiles, which are devoured ravenously in a raw state. [21]

John Wood, en route to California, left an excellent account of the activities at the fort under the date of 19 July 1850.

In this valley there is a fort, called Fort Bridger, after the old pioneer who built it and lives there near where we have camped. This valley is certainly very rich and affords the best grass; it is watered by seven beautiful streams running through it called Rushing Creeks. These streams are from ten to twenty feet wide, and from one to three feet deep of clear cold water rush from the mountain tops. The fort is occupied by a number of French and Indians of the Snake Tribe, who live well and prosper by trading. The Chief article they have to trade are furs, moccasins, whiskey, milk, buckskin pantaloons, and etc.; they sell milk at ten cents a pint and whiskey at two dollars per pint. They have hundreds of very fine cattle and horses, which the Indians take a great delight in riding. This is the only place I have seen for many hundred miles, that is fit for the abode of man, and this is truly beautiful; here the wild rose and wild flowers flourish and bloom in all their varieties, and green grows the willow on the banks of the ice cold streams of Rushing Creeks, while all around are towering snow capped mountains shooting their tops high up in heaven, presenting at once an appearance to the beholder, perfectly sublime and enrapturing.

July 20, 1850—This morning we are told that over one hundred lodges of Indians are to meet here today, at the fort to exhibit five thousand horses, a prize they have taken from the Utah tribe, with whom they have been at war. They must have fought a good fight, and I should be very glad to stay here today and see them exhibit their trophies of war, but something seems to say stay not till to-morrow's sun. [22]

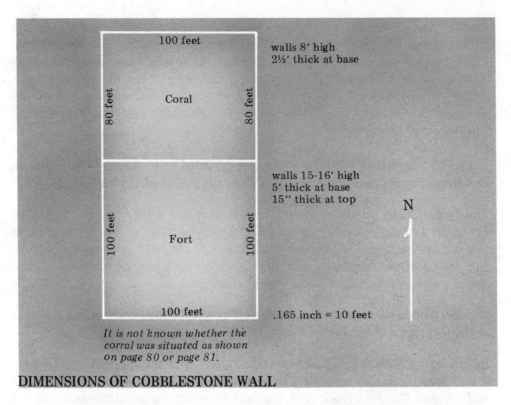

DIMENSIONS OF COBBLESTONE WALL

One of the reasons for the poor condition of the fort in 1850 could have been the marriage of Bridger to his third wife. Bridger, who had lost his second wife in July 1849, married again in 1850 to a woman of the Snake tribe, and soon after bought a small farm near Little Sante Fe, Missouri, and removed there with his family from Fort Bridger that same year. With his family living in the East most of the time Bridger had little interest in the upkeep of the fort. Vasquez was spending much of his time going to and from Salt Lake City, where he was planning to open a mercantile store. Since he was looked upon by the Mormons as one who could be trusted, his activities in Salt Lake City were not hindered.

On 23 July 1853 Harriet Sherrill Ward arrived at Fort Bridger. She recorded the following item in her diary:

A mile from our encampment we came to Fort Bridger of which we had a fine view from the road which ran about a mile west of it. The grounds in the immediate vicinity of the fort were green and beautiful although I could discover no trace of cultivation. The fort is built of adobes but I am unable to give minute description of it, not being near enough to see it distinctly.[23]

The statement that the fort was built of adobes was an error but may be explained by Dr. Thomas Flint's description on 27 August 1853. Flint said:

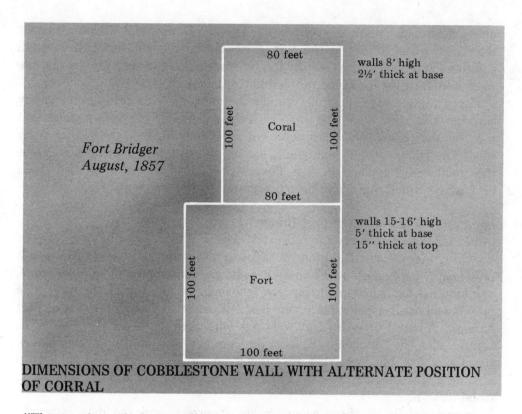

80 feet

walls 8' high
2½' thick at base

100 feet

Coral

100 feet

*Fort Bridger
August, 1857*

80 feet

walls 15-16' high
5' thick at base
15" thick at top

100 feet

Fort

100 feet

100 feet

DIMENSIONS OF COBBLESTONE WALL WITH ALTERNATE POSITION OF CORRAL

"The fort is made by setting in the ground two parallel lines of high posts and filling in between with gravelly clay."[24] The gravelly clay between the picket walls could have very easily been mistaken by Mrs. Ward as adobe since she was making her description from a distance of about one mile. All the other references to the fort describe it as a single picket wall. On 6 August 1853, twenty-one days before Flint's arrival, Frederick H. Piercy stopped at the fort and recorded his impression of the fort as being

. . . merely a trading post, then belonging to Major James Bridger one of the oldest mountaineers in this region. The fort is built in the usual form of pickets, with lodging apartments opening into a hollow square. A high picket fence encloses a yard into which the animals of the establishment are driven for protection, both from wild beasts and Indians. Mr. Bridger had erected a board on which was written a request for emigrants to keep a mile away from his place. [25]

The description of the fort's walls is a mystery. It is possible the walls had always been as Flint describes but very unlikely. There had been too many excellent descriptions of the fort since 1843 to have overlooked such a feature. Perhaps the walls had been fortified for additional strength and the descriptions of the fort since that time of remodeling had been overlooked. It is possible the newly described walls were erected in 1848 when Bridger and Vasquez brought their new wives to live at the fort. It should be remembered that in 1848 additions were made to the fort by its owners and it could very well be that the walls were fortified for added protection for the families.

Piercy's statement concerning the sign is interesting. Had Bridger completely withdrawn in 1853 from any trade with the emigrants? It is very possible that this was the reason Mrs. Ward never got any closer to the fort than the main road. The majority of the emigrants passing the fort were Mormons which at this point could explain the sign. Possibly, too, Bridger was concerned about his pastures which could have been overgrazed by the emigrants' stock.

Mormon Reconstruction of Fort Bridger

Concerning the reconstruction of Fort Bridger, Coutant stated in his *History of Wyoming* that "Louis Robison rebuilt it in 1855, and when it was finished it presented a very substantial appearance. It was constructed of boulder stone, one hundred feet square and fourteen feet high. On the top of the walls were pickets and on diagonal corners were bastions, somewhat after the style of Fort Laramie. A corral fifty-two feet wide was built against the fort." [26] Milton R. Hunter adds the following, "During the summer of 1855, the Mormons constructed a few buildings at Fort Bridger and a heavy wall of cobblestone masonery was erected. This replaced the original picket wall of logs which stood on end." [27]

Several details of these accounts are incorrect, and the date is wrong, for as of April 1857 Lewis Robison had not started the construction of the fort. In writing to Daniel H. Wells during that month, Robison said: "The President spoke of my forting in. I would like to know his mind about what size fort to make also what length and what thickness of wall. The present fort is about 80 feet square." [28]

In a second letter written to Daniel H. Wells on May 30, 1857, Robison declared:

In the first place I have laid out the Fort 100 feet square in the clear and the horse corral joining on the North 80 feet by 100 feet, which I am putting up a wall 2½ feet thick at the bottom and 8 feet high. I wish to know the Presidents view with repair to gates, port holes and also to know how I am to pay the hands that are laboring for me. Thus far I have payed them mostly in flour. If it would not be asking too much I would like to have a draft of the Fort frame as he would like to have it built and sent to me. I have no Mason here except Jerome Thempton and I hardly think him competent to put up the fort as it should be done. If you could send a good mason out to boss the work I would be glad. [29]

Again two weeks later Robison wrote Brigham Young stating: "I have got my horse corral finished except the gates and am getting along quite well with

82

the fort. The north wall is up 16 feet high and we will nearly finish the west line tomorrow."[30] This was confirmed by Orson Pratt's diary of August 14, which reported the following: "Spend 14th of Aug at Fort Bridger Brother Lewis Robison in charge of the station and just completed the wall of the new fort built of rock in mortor."[31]

Two days earlier John Pulsipher wrote in his diary that "Brother Robison made feast and dance, invited us all to celebrate the completion of the new Fort Bridger. Strong walls 16 feet high and five feet thick."[32] Tragically, events were developing that would cause Robison to burn the fort to the ground just two months after the completion of the new additions. The cause was the approach of Johnston's Army in the fall of 1857.

7

Arrival at Fort Bridger was a welcome rest for many weary handcart emigrants.

Mormons occupy—then destroy Fort Bridger

The Changing Role for Fort Bridger

With the Mormon purchase of Fort Bridger in 1855, the role of the outpost changed once again. Serving as a haven for trappers and traders during the declining years of the fur trade, the fort experienced renewed life as an oasis for the travelers crossing the continent, and then became one of the most prominent emigrant trading posts in the western United States. Now it became a supply station for Mormon emigrants en route to Salt Lake Valley.

Where Bridger and Vasquez had encouraged emigrants to follow the Oregon Trail west by way of Fort Bridger, Mormon owners reversed this policy. They actually discouraged non-Mormon emigrants from traveling via Fort Bridger because of limited supplies at the fort. Instead, they suggested the several cutoffs to Fort Hall. In letters to Lewis Robison, Brigham Young often commented on the satisfaction of the Church leaders knowing that the emigrants were not traveling via Fort Bridger.

The beginning of much-needed improvements on Fort Bridger in 1855 and actual reconstruction in 1857 was partly a result of the plans of Church leaders to give Fort Bridger a key role in a Mormon communications, transportation and freighting system. As early as November 1855 the Church had proposed the establishment of a water freight line up the Missouri to Fort Union and up the Yellowstone River. From there the goods could be freighted to Fort Bridger along the Mormon Trail. But by 1856 a major program was being developed which included planned communities every twenty miles between the Missouri River and Salt Lake Valley, which would give the Mormons control over the freighting and transportation of goods and people to Salt Lake Valley, and would serve as way stations for the Mormon emigrant trains—especially the handcart companies. The Brigham Young Express and Carrying Company, called the B.Y.X. Co., organized and made calls to establish stations along the route between Independence and Salt Lake City. They made plans to strengthen the outposts already established at Fort Bridger and Fort Supply.

It was this plan that inspired Brigham Young's successful attempt to obtain the overland mail contract with the low bid of $23,000, made possible by the existence of the B.Y.X. Co. Unfortunately for the Mormons, the coming of the federal army upset the plan and caused the Mormons to lose thousands of dollars that had been invested in the project.

Indian Activities around Fort Bridger, 1855-1857

The fort played an important role as the headquarters for the Mormon missionary work among the Shoshone and Bannock Indians. Missionaries would not simply come and go from the fort in missionary activities, but hold meetings with local tribes there. The fort also had to be maintained as a trading post so that the physical needs of the Indians could be met as a means of gaining the friendship and confidence necessary to promote missionary work.

Lewis Robison was licensed as an Indian trader under the requirements of territorial law on 20 October 1855 by appearing with his partner Silas Richards before Brigham Young, Superintendent of Indian Affairs, paying $2,000, and receiving a license which stated they were now allowed

... to trade with the various tribes of Indians located in Green River County this Territory, and ... to carry on the business of trading with the aforesaid Indians at these various locations in the aforesaid county for the term of two years from the date hereof, and to keep in his employ thereat, the following named persons, or any of them in the capacities affixed to their names respectively to write, all of which persons, I am satisfied from my own knowledge, sustain a fair character and are fit to be in the Indian country. Given under my hand and seal this 20th day of October Eighteen hundred and Fifty five.

Brigham Young
Govr and Ex officio Supt of
Indian Affairs U. Territory [1]

It is interesting to note that Brigham Young was satisfied from his "own knowledge" that Lewis Robison "sustained a fair character" and was "fit to be in the Indian Country." Two years earlier, James Bridger had lost his license to trade with the Indians at Fort Bridger because Superintendent Young believed he was lacking in proper character traits.

W. H. Jackson photograph of Washakie's encampment in foothills near the fort.

In October 1855 Governor Young issued a proclamation concerning necessary steps that must be taken to maintain peace with the Indians in the Fort Bridger area. An Indian uprising which led to the proclamation was provoked by mountaineers in their last effort to vent their feelings against the Mormons in that area. Apparently realizing that the Mormons were moving in in strength, the mountain men ceased to opposed them openly.

The Mormons were hopeful that with the coming of the spring peaceful relationships could be established and strengthened with the Indians and that the Indians would recognize the purchase of the fort and accept the establishment of the two Mormon settlements upon their lands. By April 1856 it was apparent that their hopes were realized. Lewis Robison arrived in Salt Lake City from Fort Bridger on 8 April 1856 and reported the "peaceful relationships with the Indians in that quarter." Again on 17 April 1856 the governor received news by mail brought in from Fort Bridger, "that the Indians were quiet in that region."

In late June 1856, Isaac Bullock, writing from Fort Supply to Brigham Young, removed the fears in the minds of the Mormon leaders in regard to the

Indians' acceptance of the additional settlement of Mormons upon their lands. Bullock reported that "Wash-i-keek was glad for their presence." In reply, Brigham Young stated:

We are glad that Wash-i-keek and his band feel so well satisfied in regards to our settling upon his land. Let all the brethren pursue a uniform course toward them of friendship and peace, continue to conciliate them, and force them by your kinship to love you. This not only will gain but maintain peace and good will toward each other.[2]

The Mormon leader was quick to capitalize on the peaceful nature of the Shoshone under the leadership of Washakie. In a letter written on 11 August 1856 in his capacity as superintendent of Indian affairs, Young advised William Hickman to meet with the Shoshone Indians and

. . . hold a council with Wash-i-kik and his principal men, during which you will endeavor to inculcate friendly feelings and give such instruction as shall have a tendency to induce the Indians to abandon their wandering and predatory mode of life, and induce them to cultivate the earth, and raise stock for a subsistance. You will also seek to impress upon their minds the benefits of civilized existence, and of their locating themselves so that schools may be established among them. You will seek to conciliate them toward each other and with other tribes as well as toward the whites with whom however it is believed they have ever been at peace and friendly. . . . In the distribution of the presents you will collect as many of the Indians together at Fort Bridger as you can and call to your aid Mr. Lewis Robison of that place and Mr. Isaac Bullock of Fort Supply.[3]

Just a week later the Mormon leaders in the Bridger area, Hickman, Bullock, and Robison, were able to report a successful council with the Shoshone chief and his leading men in the following letter signed by William A. Hickman, Isaac Bullock, and Lewis Robison:[4]

Fort Bridger Green River County U.T. Aug. 19-1856
To Pres. B. Young

Dear Bro. Sir:

We address you a few lines to inform you of the intercourse we have had with Wash-i-kik and his tribe. There were present 40 lodges, 300 persons. On the arrival of the Indian goods at Fort Bridger, pr. William A. Hickman, Isaac Bullock of Fort Supply sent Joshua Terry in search of Washikik and his band, found them high up on Bear River on the eve of starting to this place. Terry

88

informed that Wm. A. Hickman was at Bridger with presents for them. On the 16th Wash-i-kik and his band arrived here. We smoked, had dinner and gave them a beef, after which we had a treaty or Council with Wash-i-kik and some 15 of his braves, explained the nature of Hickman's coming and by whom sent. A good spirit seemed to prevail and after much conversation adjourned till next day at which time Wash-i-kik was notified that he should have another beef, and also his presents as sent by Gov. Young per Wm. A. Hickman, and that Isaac Bullock seemed to render good satisfaction to all the Indians present. . . .

The letter also contained a description of the distribution of the presents the following morning and commented favorably on the friendliness of Washakie and his people and especially on the order that prevailed during the presentation of the gifts and the long speech by Chief Washakie.

This orderly conduct did not always prevail as evidenced in a letter sent by Robison to Daniel H. Wells just four days later. Robison reported that Washakie and "a large amount of his people came to the fort . . . to have a spree." The Mormon leader attempted to intervene in a fight between Washakie and one of his tribesmen named Razease, and was hit "several times in the face" by Washakie. Robison then tried to close the store, but Washakie forced him to stay open and supply him and his favorites with whiskey, resulting in an all-day drinking bout. The Mormon storekeeper estimated that they consumed twenty gallons of liquor before Washakie pronounced that "they should drink no more." [5]

The next morning the Indians quarreled over a proposed attack on the Utes. Washakie opposed the action, but became enraged at his mother's defiance of his orders and stabbed her in the side with a butcher knife. Some of the braves proposed to kill Washakie for the rash act, but it was decided to wait to see if the wounded lady died. The Shoshone chief left the post with his family, and Robison reported that Washakie's mother was still alive three days after the altercation.

This incident revealed a different side of Washakie's character, and indicated the need for patience, diplomacy and judgment on the part of the officials who were dealing with him. Lewis Robison seemed to have had many of the qualities needed to work with the Indians of the region.

Brigham Young, in his triple role of Governor, Indian Superintendent, and Church President, felt that the expenses incurred should be borne by the U.S. Government. His letter to George W. Manypenny, Commissioner of Indian Affairs, requested payment but did not indicate who had distributed the gifts:

Enclosed two drafts one for $840 in favor of Joseph F. Mason of Weston, Mo., and one for $3,756.50 in favor of Levi Stewart and Co. of Great Salt Lake City.

The above amounts have arisen through the necessity of making purchases of certain presents for the Shoshonee Indians, and have the fullest sanction of my judgment as to the most judicious management of the affairs of this Super-intendency as far as that tribe is at present concerned.[6]

It is apparent that the bill of $4,596.50 was paid by the Commissioner of Indian Affairs. Yet the presents received there by the Indians were distributed by the three Mormon leaders in the region, Hickman, Bullock, and Robison. It seems likely that the Indians believed that the presents and supplies came from the Mormons. In fact, Lewis Robison, writing to Daniel H. Wells concerning the council held with the Indians, stated:

. . . the council with the Shoshoneys has gone off first rate and to our entire satisfaction so far as I have knowledge of the transaction hear. I presume much better than If Armstrong [the Indian subagent in the region] *had been here.*[7]

There is little doubt that the Mormon colonies were the chief beneficiaries of the council with Washakie, but the peaceful relations established were beneficial to all the occupants of the region.

Indian relations at Fort Bridger were quiet during the remaining months of 1856 and into the early summer of 1857. In the latter part of June, Washakie and a small party of Shoshones visited the fort. Robison wrote, "they feel first rate towards us, a more friendly feeling I never have seen manifested among the Indians." Soon after Washakie and his band left, a war party of Arapahos numbering forty braves visited the fort. They had been warring against the Utes under the leadership of their famous chief, Friday. Robison described the Arapahos as "the finest looking Indians that I ever have seen. They had a good interpreter with them belonging to the nation so we had a good chance to talk with them." Continuing, Robison recorded:

. . . as a matter of course they were very hungry. I killed a beef for them and gave them some flour and other things. They were anxious to have me meet them on Plat River at the mouth of Sweetwater to trade this coming winter. They say next year they are coming to the valley with their big chief to see the President.[8]

The Mormon-Indian relations at Fort Bridger remained peaceful during the summer of 1857. Prior to the coming of the Federal army in the fall of 1857, which disrupted the trade and missionary activities between the Mormons and Indians, Brigham Young's plan of using Fort Bridger as a base of operations in accomplishing his goals with the Indians was meeting with success.

Mormon Life at Fort Bridger

According to Lewis Robison, life at Fort Bridger "is very dull at times here. I scarcely get to see a dime and when I do it is pinched out of . . . shape."[9]

President Buchanan was responsible for sending army troops to Utah Territory.

Robison's wife and young children spent considerable time in Salt Lake Valley with her family to escape the boredom of the fort, since for the majority of the time they were the only whites residing there.

But there was no lack of things to do in the line of physical labor. The effort needed to stay alive and to maintain the settlement for the Church demanded many hours of work with the crops, the animals, and the supplies for trade.

There was the opportunity on occasion to enjoy the social advantages of Fort Supply only twelve miles away, yet this was hampered by the friction generated when Robison was unsuccessful in getting men at Fort Supply to do work at Fort Bridger for wages. Robison wrote:

I have tried to get some hands from Fort Supply, but have not as yet got any. They think that a dollar a day and bread is not enough. And would rather go on the road to trade with the emigrants, (where there is two traders to one emigrant already on the road). [10]

Upon hearing word of the problem Robison was having with men at Fort Supply, Brigham Young was quoted in a letter written by Daniel H. Wells to Lewis Robison as follows:

The President would like to have you take the names of such men as go out on the road to trade also as such as will not work without such high wages he would like to know if this course is approved by the President Isaac Bullock. [11]

91

The majority of time was spent at the fort in maintaining a surplus of food and supplies for the emigrant trains en route to the valley, and keeping stocked the supplies needed for trade with the Indians. Fort Bridger kept a considerable amount of goods in order to greatly reduce the amount of food to be freighted by emigrants coming from the Missouri River. Emigrants often sent couriers ahead to have supplies sent back to meet them, and to request that there be enough provided for them upon arrival at the fort.

The following excerpts from letters written at Fort Bridger to Salt Lake City are typical of the hundreds written in regard to supplies:

I am out of tobacco and would like to have you send me some if you think best. Two kinds the best and the poorest, the cheapest you have is good for Indian trade. I received eleven rifles from George Knollton, which is in very bad condition. They were boxed within a box made of green boards. Badly rusted and nothing in the box to keep them from rubbing together so you can judge they are in poor condition for trade.[12]

Another:

We are nearly out of liquor and as that is all that certainly brings cash I think it would be well to get an order on some of the merchant trains to leave some here for this post.[13]

And again:

I have but little amunition left and I am entirely out of knives for Indian trade. My stock of food also is nearly out. Is it best for me to send teams to the valley for flour or will there be a chance to send it out cheaper than I can send for it.[14]

In answer to Robison's request for flour the following was written: "If you have spare teams and can get teamsters prepared you had better send for your flour and at the same time bring in a wagon or two left at that point loaded with iron."[15]

Fort Bridger, as mentioned previously, was closely linked with emigration and communications. Consequently, the life at the fort was centered around maintaining and providing for these needs. Concerning the role of Fort Bridger as a mail station, Lewis Robison reported that the mail came in through Fort Bridger and that the mail company left their animals to be cared for at the fort, but the company never paid its debts:

They say that their will be an agent up the next trip to pay up the debts on the line. I cannot place much confidence in what they say. You may probably hear something from Washington that you may be able to ascertain when they will be likely to pay their debts or not. If so, please inform me and what course I had best take at the earliest opportunity.[16]

It seems apparent that the Mormon Church did not receive the money owed by the mail company. In July 1856 Brigham Young wrote Lewis Robison telling him to quit caring for their animals. In response to Young's letter, Robison wrote the following:

Dodsen came out with a letter from the President to me requesting me to withdraw the attention of the mail animals (which I have done). Also to forward my account against the mail company to his office at the first convenient opportunity. Enclosed you will find an order on Hooper and William for the full amount of their indebtedness to me amounting to about $900.[17]

The work involved with the emigration into Salt Lake Valley from late spring to late fall kept Robison busy. Mormons gained ownership of Fort Bridger just a year before the first of the handcart trains made its way to Utah. By the time they reached Fort Bridger, they were in most cases in poor, if not destitute, condition. The Fort played a major role in the rescue of late companies led by Martin and Willie which were caught in a heavy snowstorm in early October 1856 near present day Casper, Wyoming. An estimated two hundred of the one thousand emigrants lost their lives, and it is likely that many more would have suffered the same fate if Fort Bridger had not been available as a source of supplies as well as a haven for rescued and rescuers alike.

A letter written by Lewis Robison to Brigham Young indicates the level of activity at the fort when an emigration train arrived: "This is Sunday all though it does not seem much like it here. . . . [It] has been quite a busy day as there has been emigration passing through everyday."[18]

In connection with the emigration, Robison was to provide new stock for emigrants to be traded for their worn-out animals which would be rested, fed and cared for at Fort Bridger, and then traded for other animals to come later in the season. Caring for these animals and getting them back into shape took considerable time. Robison wrote: "The wolves are still very bad, they have killed three head of cattle since spring and have pulled off the bags of two cows within a few days past."[19] Because of the large number of animals accumulated over the summer months, feed was hard to find. This posed the problem for Robison of finding added pasture. "I think that we shall have to take our stock off of the ranch to winter." Robison mentioned another constant problem: "the horse flies, gnats and mosquitoes are very troublesome indeed; our stock is not yet improving much in flesh."

Because of the large amount of livestock, it was Robison's duty to grow as much feed as possible to cut down expenses. Thus, during the warm months farming became a major part of life at the fort. A person had to live only one year at Fort Bridger or Fort Supply to discover the difficulty of growing crops due to the unpredictable weather and hordes of grasshoppers. Concerning the killing cold spell, he wrote, "the season still remains cold and backwards, the 4th inst. [May] it snowed all day long as hard as they ever make it and it had not yet gone off." Later he recorded that, "the seasons is quite cold, on the night of the 10th inst. [July] the frost cut my potatoes to the ground, they were in bloom and looked well." [20]

Grasshoppers presented a major problem as evidenced by Robison's note to Daniel H. Wells reporting that

... the grasshoppers have nearly destroyed my garden and have injured the crops very much. ... The crops look very well where the grasshoppers have not taken it. The grasshoppers are nearly grown and we feel in hopes they will soon emigrate. [21]

Life at Fort Bridger at best was difficult for the Mormon colonists. For most food items and supplies they depended upon freight from Salt Lake City. The constant pressure for the safety of the emigrants and the hard physical life necessary for survival did not make living easy. With the association of only the emigrants, the occasional visitors from Salt Lake Valley, such as church authorities, or missionaries en route to or from missions, and the Indians (sometimes more trouble than company), there must have been lonely days. There was no social life whatsoever except a rare visit to friends at Fort Supply. It was little wonder the women and children spent considerable time in the valley, and Lewis Robison referred to Fort Bridger as dull.

The Burning of Fort Bridger and Fort Supply
So many complaints of misunderstanding, suspicion, malice, and troubles in the Utah Territory had filtered into Washington that in the 1857 session of Congress President Buchanan pointed out that the supremacy of the United States in that region must be restored and maintained. He therefore appointed Alfred Cumming to replace Brigham Young as Governor and ordered Cumming and other federal officers to proceed to Utah accompanied by a large military escort.

General William S. Harney was to take command of the escort but he was detained by political troubles in Kansas. The forces consisting of the First, Seventh, and Tenth Infantries, and Second Dragoons, along with the Phelps and Reno batteries of the Fourth Artillery, all began their westward march on July 18, each under its own officers without a unified command. The late start brought criticism and led to the forecast that the troops could not reach Fort Laramie before winter. Colonel E. B. Alexander of the Tenth Infantry was the senior officer among the troops, but he did not assume command of the entire force until October.

The army moved without difficulty westward over the well-beaten Oregon Trail toward South Pass. On September 28, Colonel Alexander and his Tenth Infantry reached Ham's Fork near the Green River in Utah Territory, and set up Camp Winfield to await the arrival of the other detachments.

Colonel Alexander received a military proclamation from Governor Young on September 15, in which Young forbade the entry of armed forces into Utah Territory. He also received a letter from Brigham Young written September 29 stating that the troops could winter in the area of Black's Fork unmolested, providing they would turn their weapons over to the Utah territorial quartermaster and would leave in the spring. Alexander's reply was that the "troops are here by order of the President of the United States, and their future movements and operations will depend entirely upon orders issued by competent military officers." [22] Brigham Young, determined to keep the army from entering Utah, called out the territorial militia and assigned some units to occupy the narrow Echo Canyon route into the Mormon area. Other units were assigned to disrupt the approaching army by destroying army supplies. The units were told to stampede all army animals, burn all grass before and around them, keep the troops awake by night surprises, blockade roads with rock and fallen trees, destroy fords in streams and envelop trains with prairie fires set to their windward.

Eleven days after Brigham Young received word of the approaching army, he wrote to Lewis Robison at Fort Bridger stating that he did not expect the army to give the settlers at the forts any trouble that season. He felt that the U.S. troops probably would not get as far as Fort Laramie, but that if they did, they would remain there during the winter. [23]

> *Presidents Office*
> *Great Salt Lake City*
> *August 4th, 1857*

Lewis Robison Esq.
Fort Bridger

Dear Brother:
> *Your note by Mr. Gillim came to hand today. We are glad to hear from you and trust that you will do well. We are all well and peace and prosperity attends all our efforts.*
> *The most interesting item afloat at present is the reported expedition of Gen. Harney against us. We do not intend to be taken this time, but we think they will not reach Fort Laramie this year, and then something will probably turn up to give them another direction. Be this as it may they will not be permitted to come into this Territory to plunder, rob and murder as seems to be their wishes and designs.*

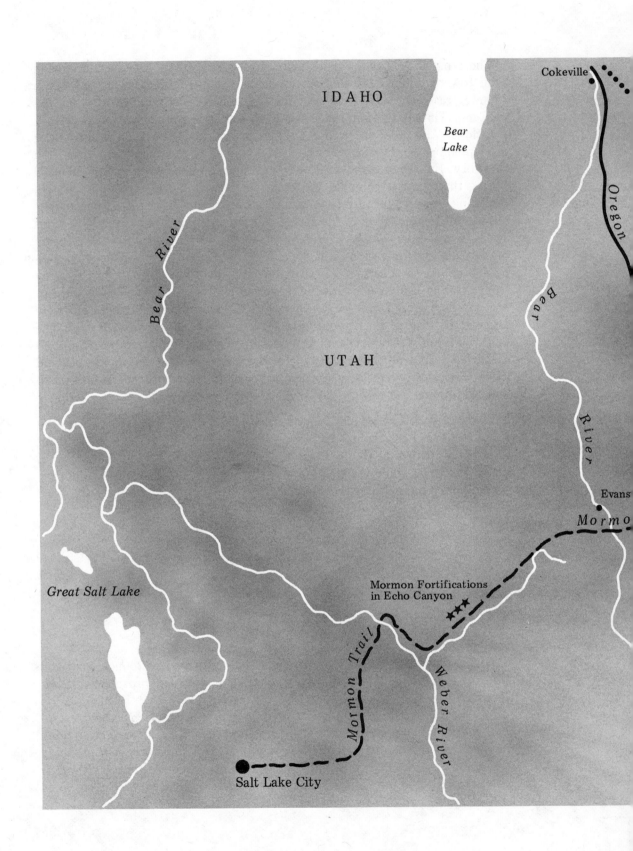

IDAHO

Bear Lake

UTAH

Bear River

Bear River

Oregon

Cokeville

Evans

Mormo

Great Salt Lake

Mormon Fortifications
in Echo Canyon

Mormon Trail

Weber River

Salt Lake City

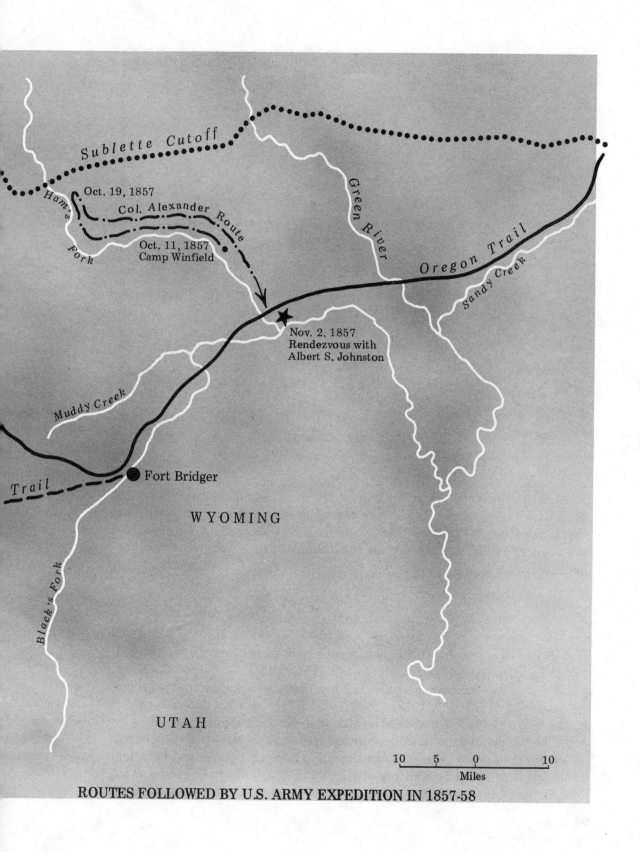

Sublette Cutoff

Ham's Fork

Oct. 19, 1857

Col. Alexander Route

Oct. 11, 1857
Camp Winfield

Green River

Oregon Trail

Sandy Creek

Nov. 2, 1857
Rendezvous with
Albert S. Johnston

Muddy Creek

Trail

Fort Bridger

WYOMING

Black's Fork

UTAH

10   5   0   10
Miles

ROUTES FOLLOWED BY U.S. ARMY EXPEDITION IN 1857-58

Orin P. Rockwell led Mormon guerrilla bands against army supply trains.

. . . But [obtain] of the emigration all the guns and ammunition that you can at reasonable prices, although we expect to make our enemies furnish us what we shall need of those articles . . . that is if they come near enough to give us a chance, and if they do not we shall not need it. . . . Fix your guns for shooting but lay low.

As ever yours,
Brigham Young

Even as late as September 7, Brigham Young gave assurance to Lewis Robison that the settlers at the fort would be safe that winter. He believed the army would not go beyond Fort Laramie. But he encouraged the colonists to allow the passage of U.S. supply trains. These could be possessed as partial payment for the debt owed to the territorial legislature by the federal government.

By the middle of September the Fort Bridger and Fort Supply settlers began to fear for their safety. The U.S. Army received Brigham Young's proclamation forbidding it to enter the territory at Ham's Fork, only thirty-five miles from Fort Bridger. Orders were now being given to the people at the forts that they

98

must hold back the army and not permit it to pass. Tight security was being placed on all individuals seeking entrance into the valley.

> *Utah Territory*
> *Government Office*
> *September 16th*

Salt Lake City
Lewis Robison Esq.
Fort Bridger

Dear Sir:

Mess. Rouh [sic] and Jones are going out to the Government trains we send out a few of the proclamations declaring Martial Law.

The trains at Ham Fork must not be permitted to come any further in this direction, neither do we expect that any more trains will be permitted to come this side of the pass, stop their progress by stampeding their cattle, but save the lives of men as much as possible.

We have written to Bro. Isaac Bullock to the same effect. We wish you and him to use what power you have to carry out these purposes in connection with Bro. Cummings and Burton you and Bro. Bullock are authorized to give permits for people to pass and repass to and from. Examine all strangers and suspected persons strictly before you grant permits.

> *Your Friend and Brother*
> *Brigham Young*
> *Governor and Ex Officio*
> *Supt. of Indian Affairs*
> *U. T.*[24]

The exact date the settlers began to leave Fort Bridger and Fort Supply by the order of Brigham Young is not known, but by September 29 the majority of the families were bound for Salt Lake City. George A. Smith, on his way east with a military expedition, reported that "on the 29th of September, I met some fifty families fleeing from Fort Supply and Fort Bridger, with ox and horse teams, and their herds of cattle bound for Great Salt Lake City."[25]

Upon deserting their property in Green River County, the settlers burned all their buildings and fields. They did not want to leave supplies that would aid the army, which to them was the threat "of an armed mob."

During the evening of October 2, Lewis Robison set fire to Fort Bridger. The torch was set to Fort Supply around midnight of the same day. Jesse W. Crosby, one of the Mormons who participated in the campaign against Johnston's Army, reported:

Lot Smith, prominent figure in Mormon raids against U.S. Army supply wagons.

100

The company to which I belonged left Salt Lake City September 25, 1857. We took out our wagons, horses, etc., and at twelve o'clock set fire to the buildings [Fort Supply] at once, consisting of one hundred or more good hewed log houses, one sawmill, one gristmill and one thrashing machine, and after going out of the fort we set fire to the stockade work, straw and grain stacks, etc. After looking a few minutes at the bonfire we had made, thence on by the light thereof. I will mention that owners of property in several places begged the privilege of setting fire to their own, which they freely did, thus destroying at once what they had labored for years to build and that without a word. We then went our way a few miles and stopped to set fire to the City Supply, a new place just commenced; there were ten or fifteen buildings perhaps, and warmed ourselves by the flames. Thus was laid waste in a few hours all the labor of a settlement for three or four years, with some five or six hundred acres of land fenced and improved.

Our work of destruction was now finished and we moved silently onward and reached Bridger a little after daylight and found it in ashes, it having been fired the night before.[26]

Four years of colonizing efforts in the Green River Valley were left in ashes, bringing to a close the Mormon control of Fort Bridger. With the army's arrival in November of 1857, Colonel Johnston took possession of the fort in the name of the United States and declared it to be a military reservation. The reservation was also extended over the settlement and farming lands of Fort Supply.

There are varying estimates of the amount of money the Mormons lost because of the fire, and the possession of the fort by the Federal Army. Milton R. Hunter states: "The total loss and damage sustained by these Mormon Pioneers in this case [was] about $300,000." Another Mormon source reported, "The estimated amount of the property thus destroyed at Fort Bridger was $2,000, at Fort Supply, $50,000."

At first glance, the latter estimate might appear to be reasonable, but in light of the figures given in Crosby's account of the number of homes, buildings, and acreage destroyed at Fort Supply, plus the homes and acreage of Supply City and Fort Bridger, the estimate of $300,000 is certainly acceptable, if not a bit conservative. The figure of $2,000 for the loss of Fort Bridger is certainly in error, because the appraised value of Fort Bridger before the construction of the wall was $11,800.

If the figure of $300,000 is used to represent the amount lost by the Mormons at Fort Bridger and Fort Supply, and if one adds on the $49,953.10 spent by the Mormons in disbursements to the Nauvoo Legion (the Mormon name for the territorial militia) plus the $1,998.11 worth of supplies furnished by Lewis Robison at Fort Bridger, the legion's attempt to keep the U.S. Army out of Salt Lake Valley was as expensive as it was risky.

8

A magazine illustrator made this sketch of the fort's military occupation.

Johnston's army shivers in burned-out Fort Bridger

When the Mormons decided to burn Fort Bridger and retreat from the Green River region, leaving it to the oncoming U.S. Army, they set the stage for one of the most dramatic periods in the history of the fort. The initial year of army occupation was especially bizarre.

Although the post had been burned and abandoned early in October 1857, the army did not actually occupy the area until mid-November. Colonel Edmund Alexander, the temporary commander of the military force, had established a temporary post on Ham's Fork of the Green River, some twenty-five miles northeast of Fort Bridger. It was there that Captain Van Vliet, the army's advance agent who was returning from Salt Lake City, informed Colonel Alexander that the Mormons intended to resist if the army attempted to enter the Mormon stronghold. Alexander, apprehensive about attempting to force his way through narrow Echo Canyon, then decided to wait for the arrival of the newly appointed commanding officer, Colonel Albert Sidney Johnston. However, in the early part of October, when the Mormon guerrilla bands under the leadership of Lot Smith, Robert Burton, and others were successful in burning several of the supply trains and in driving off the cattle and horses belonging to Alexander's units, he found himself in a somewhat desperate situation. On October 6 he called a council of war and decided to follow the old trappers' route into the Salt Lake Valley. The army would move to the northwest up Ham's Fork, then turn west to the Bear River, following it to the northern

Albert S. Johnston, army commander.   *Randolph Marcy, military officer.*

border of Utah where several broad and unfortified valleys led directly into the Mormon settlements.

After completing final preparations, according to Norman F. Furniss,[1] "the army began its march on October 11. For three days the column, seven miles long from the Tenth Infantry in the van to the Fifth Infantry at the rear, made fair progress along Ham's Fork. Morale of the troops was high despite the presence of Mormons in the nearby hills. Although the weather was cold and the road rough, the men were healthy and seemed delighted to be moving again after so many stagnant days."

This apparently pleasant situation was soon changed when within three days the road became nearly impassable, the weather became colder, and on October 17 a snowstorm arrived halting the army only thirty-five miles out of Camp Winfield. "At this point Colonel Alexander began to doubt the soundness of his decision to follow the Bear River route into Utah; however, he permitted his men to remain in their camp for another eight days before moving." It was at this time that commanding officer Colonel Johnston finally made contact and ordered Alexander to meet him at Ham's Fork. "The soldiers and their four thousand animals struggled down Ham's Fork to the place of rendezvous chosen by their commander. Badly worn, they arrived there on November 2. Having gained nothing by their exertions of the past weeks, they had returned

104

Alfred Cumming, Utah governor. *Territorial justice, Delana Eccles.*

to a camp with pitifully inadequate forage and dangerously low temperatures." Johnston immediately saw that his present location would not suffice for winter quarters, and decided to push on to Fort Bridger thirty-five miles distant. "On November 6 the troops began the desperate race for the sheltered valley before the animals failed completely. Intense cold froze the feet of the dragoons on patrol, and congealed the grease on the caissons' axles. Animals, already weakened by the cold, had little to eat besides cottonwood bark and sage. The eighty horses in Phelps's battery received only twelve bushels of corn during the first eleven days of November." Cattle staggered and fell until there were no longer enough animals to move the trains. When they finally reached the remains of Fort Bridger on 18 November 1857, Johnston took careful stock of his situation. He knew that the Mormons had burned three of his supply trains and that Porter Rockwell, a Mormon guerrilla leader, had stolen eight hundred head of cattle. "Another three hundred animals had been run off by the Mormons just before the army left Ham's Fork." Alexander's futile advance up Ham's Fork and back to Bridger lost another three thousand head of cattle to starvation and cold, which left the army in a very difficult situation.

In addition to this, Lieutenant Colonel Philip St. George Cooke, who was making his way from Fort Laramie accompanied by the new governor Alfred Cumming and his wife, had not yet reached Fort Bridger. They were having a difficult trip. On November 8 when the temperature was forty-four degrees below zero, Cooke abandoned his wagons and plodded on, struggling through two feet of snow. After another week of severe cold thirty-six soldiers and teamsters were frostbitten. "Maddened by the cold and lack of food, mules destroyed the wagon tongues to which they were tied, ate away the rope, and attacked the camp tents, dying in great numbers." But Cooke was finally able to lead his group into Fort Bridger on November 20. Only fourteen of his 144 horses had survived and the morale of his men had been shaken by this experience. Johnston's army was now united in the environs of Fort Bridger, facing the terrible cold of the high altitude winter—with an alarming lack of food.

Colonel Johston made an immediate survey of the place and on November 30 wrote to his command headquarters at Fort Leavenworth giving the following description of Fort Bridger:

Fort Bridger, so called, is a high well built strong stone wall enclosing a square of 100 feet and has been appropriated for the storage of supplies for the army. . . . The addition of two lunettes now being constructed one on the southwest corner and the other on the northeast corner of a stone enclosure adjoining the main one but so high it will make it defenseable by a small force and a safe place of deposit for the public property that may be left when the army advances.[2]

These lunettes were simply fortified areas on the corners of Fort Bridger. They were described as earthworks about eighteen feet thick at the base and eight feet high, surrounded by a ditch twelve feet wide and four feet deep. The lunettes were seventy feet square and mounted with cannons. The outside edge of the ditch was defended by pointed stakes inclined outward. The lunettes were the real strongholds while the burned-out shell of Fort Bridger simply served as a place to store army supplies and secure a fortified place for protection in case of any surprise attack.

Soldiers and civilians who had come along as teamsters, sutlers, and government officials formed a rather large community in the valley with Fort Bridger as the northeastern anchor. They camped along Black's Fork for a number of miles, and the entire settlement assumed the name of Camp Scott in honor of General Winfield Scott. In addition to the 1,800 regular and volunteer soldiers in the camp there were 340 young men that had been recruited from the supply wagon trains making a total of at least 2,140 military men. There was also a handful of federal officers and their servants who lived in a strange collection of houses called Ecclesville, named after territorial chief justice Delana R. Eccles, who had come in with Colonel Cooke. This sprawling camp also contained supply trains that had survived Lot Smith's raids. There were many wagons belonging to the freighting company of Russell, Majors and Waddell, upon which the expedition would depend for its provisions. The Fifth

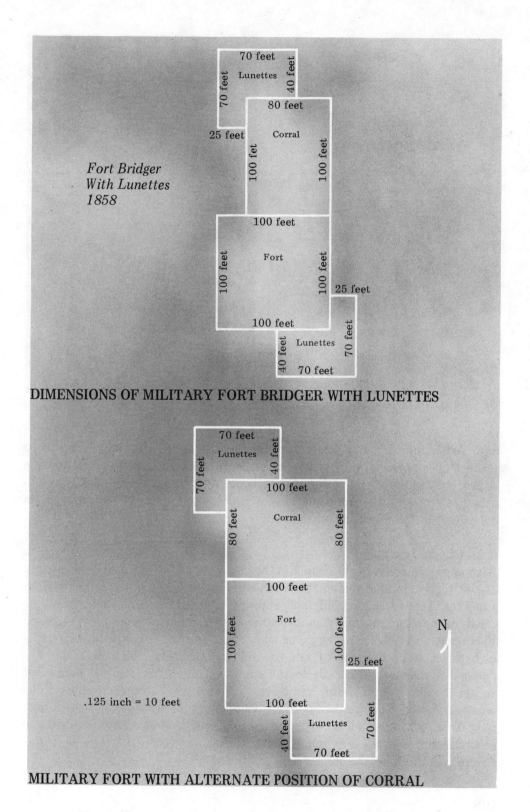

Fort Bridger
With Lunettes
1858

70 feet
Lunettes
70 feet
40 feet
25 feet
80 feet
Corral
100 feet
100 feet
100 feet
Fort
100 feet
100 feet
100 feet
25 feet
70 feet
40 feet
Lunettes
70 feet

DIMENSIONS OF MILITARY FORT BRIDGER WITH LUNETTES

70 feet
Lunettes
70 feet
40 feet
100 feet
Corral
80 feet
80 feet
100 feet
Fort
100 feet
100 feet
100 feet
25 feet
40 feet
Lunettes
70 feet
70 feet

N

.125 inch = 10 feet

MILITARY FORT WITH ALTERNATE POSITION OF CORRAL

Col. Philip Cooke escorted Cumming.   General Scott, "Old fuss 'n feathers."

and Tenth Infantry Regiments had their sutler trains drawn in a circle to protect the stock. The private mercantile firm of Livingstone and Kincade added its wagons to the scene. Camp Scott may have been hurriedly established as a makeshift winter quarters for a desperate army, but for more than half a year it was a bustling settlement.

Life at Camp Scott

With approximately 2,500 people in the camp facing the extreme cold weather of this high mountain region there was real danger of starvation or death from exposure. There was a considerable supply of bacon, ham, and flour, and some dried vegetables, but many commodities were almost impossible to obtain. There was no milk, butter, eggs, or lard. Sugar and tobacco sold at extremely high prices while the lack of salt was felt most keenly. Brigham Young dispatched a wagon load of salt to the camp but Johnston said he would not accept the gift from a traitor and turned it down. However, some enterprising troops followed Young's drivers out of camp and obtained the salt, which they were able to sell for $5.00 a pound. Several hundred bushels of turnips and other vegetables were uncovered from a Mormon cache that had been discovered. Using these, the soldiers escaped scurvy.

As the weeks dragged by the reserves dwindled in an alarming fashion. When

108

the animals began to fail because of inadequate forage, the stock was taken to Henry's Fork to winter. This forced the soldiers to haul the wagons several miles a day to bring in firewood. So long as the commissary kept the rations high men could bear the strenuous work, but when early in May the allotments were again cut, the situation became very serious. One officer, writing to the New York Tribune, said: "We are still existing but we're not living." In late November Johnston had purchased several hundred head of cattle from nearby mountain men, but by June these were almost gone. The neighboring Indians began to bring in dog meat which they offered for sale as mountain sheep. In desperation, Johnston sent word to Fort Laramie, the nearest post, describing his condition and calling on Major Hoffman to bring supplies. Hoffman complied, and though it took him until June 10 to reach Bridger, these supplies did help to restore the hungry troops and prepare them for the final march into Utah.

Another group had gone to Fort Union to try to get additional animals. Under the leadership of Captain Marcy this unit made a very courageous trip and returned with almost sixty horses and one thousand mules in spite of the very difficult journey.

In addition to the difficulties with cold and the lack of food, the commander faced the task of passing the time away with some kind of positive action. Certain military chores such as early morning drills and the like occupied the soldiers to some extent, but these exercises still left much free time during each day. For entertainment more talented soldiers erected a theatre and produced a few plays. Others formed five tents into a large ballroom where dances were held on Christmas, New Year's Eve, and a few other occasions.

Johnston reported that his troops were in excellent condition, their spirits high, and their health good, despite the fact that there was some bitterness among the officers and some real cases of insubordination among the men. Many of the soldiers spent much of the time in drinking, and a few decided to desert and slip into the Mormon country and join the enemy. Although the men in Johnston's Army fretted about the shortage of food, "they held their drills, went out on patrols in sub-zero weather, and performed the other duties of military life."[3] Johnston was an effective commander, keeping his troops under control and in a reasonable state of military preparedness.

According to Furniss, the civilian officials, marooned about one hundred yards west of Camp Scott in Ecclesville, struggled through the winter as best they could. Chief justice Eccles was a disgruntled man throughout most of this period. He knew that some of the army officers were well-housed in a new type of tent, and he bemoaned the fact that his facilities did not compare with theirs. In fact, Justice Eccles first lived in a covered hole in the ground and then in a small hut built of frozen sod. Alfred Cumming, the newly appointed governor, lived in rather grand style. He had five tents attached together which gave him room for his family and a young servant girl. Also in Ecclesville was

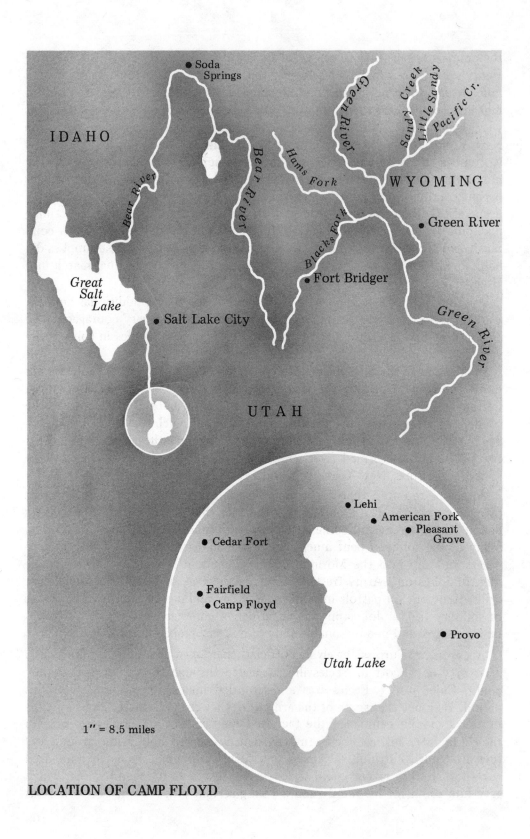

LOCATION OF CAMP FLOYD

territorial secretary John Hartnet; United States marshal Peter Dotson; territorial attorney general Jay M. Hockday; Dr. Garland Hurt, former Indian agent in Utah, and Jacob Forney who had come to replace him; postmaster H. F. Morrell; and David A. Burr, justice of the peace.[4]

One of the developments that stirred some interest in camp was the arrival of Colonel Thomas L. Kane. Kane as a young man had become acquainted with the Mormons when they were evacuating Nauvoo, and on hearing of their predicament in Utah volunteered to try to solve the difficulty. Although he was not an official representative of President Buchanan, he knew the president well and carried a letter of introduction from him and a sort of unofficial blessing for his efforts. Using the pseudonym "Dr. Osborne" he came west by way of Panama and landed in San Pedro. Stopping for a short time in the Mormon community of San Bernardino, California, he arrived in Salt Lake Valley early in March. After spending a few days in Salt Lake discussing the situation with the Mormon leaders, he was convinced that the Mormons were not in rebellion and were eager to settle the problem peaceably. Pushing on to Camp Scott, Kane arrived on 12 March 1858 too exhausted to dismount from his horse or even to speak. After resting a few days, he recovered enough to begin talking to Colonel Johnston and Governor Cumming in an attempt to resolve the difficulty.

In addition to the information concerning the Mormon attitude, Kane brought an offer from Brigham Young who promised to send fifteen or twenty thousand pounds of flour and two hundred head of cattle belonging to a Mr. Garrish, a Salt Lake merchant Young understood was now with the army at Camp Scott. Unfortunately, Kane was not a very good diplomat and he continually antagonized Johnston and others of the military. However, he did sense that Cumming was interested in making peace, and so spent most of his time working with the new governor. He finally convinced Cumming that he should go to Salt Lake Valley with a Mormon escort and investigate the situation. Governor Cumming made the trip to Salt Lake Valley early in April and three days after his arrival sent a letter to Johnston saying the Mormons were not in rebellion. He had seen the court records and found everything in order, and he reported that he was being treated respectfully and accepted as governor.

The thought that Cumming might solve the difficulties peaceably tormented the frost-bitten and hungry troops who had no desire to compromise with those who had destroyed their goods and caused them so much suffering. They had spent much of the time during the bitter winter anticipating what they would do once they got to Salt Lake with all that lovely food, and more especially, with the polygamous wives. However, the Governor's wife did much in Camp Scott to support Kane's and her husband's efforts to make peace. She was aided by Jacob Forney, the Indian superintendent, who believed that war should be avoided if possible. On the other extreme was Chief Justice Eccles,

111

T. L. Kane, self-appointed negotiator between Mormons and federal officials.

112

who was very bitter and wanted no compromise. Johnston was willing to make peace, but it had to be on his terms.

In the meantime, President Buchanan had appointed Lazarus W. Powell of Kentucky and Ben McCulloch of Texas to represent him in an effort to negotiate peace. When these men arrived in Fort Bridger on 19 May 1858 the soldiers at first greeted them sullenly, but brightened when they soon discovered that Powell and McCulloch were not instructed to negotiate with the Mormons, but rather to convince them of their folly and obtain their surrender. The peace commissioners set out for Salt Lake City on June 2, followed a day later by the anxious governor, Alfred Cumming, and the Indian agent, Jacob Forney. They found most of Salt Lake City deserted. President Young, aware that Cumming was susceptible to flattery, greeted him and his wife cordially and gave them the use of a house furnished with a piano, chairs, china, and other articles gathered from the deserted homes of the community. Forney was also given comfortable headquarters and accommodations. On the other hand, the peace commissioners had to content themselves with living in a wagon for two weeks until the Church leaders finally gave them one unfurnished room. Justice Eccles was left to sleep on the ground.[5]

A compromise settlement was finally reached, but Colonel Johnston almost upset the agreement when he decided to begin moving his army towards Salt Lake Valley before the time agreed upon. On June 13 he started his command on the road to the Mormon capital and finally arrived in Salt Lake Valley on 26 June 1858. By this time, the Mormons had deserted their principal city and had abandoned all settlements north of Salt Lake Valley, traveling south to Utah Valley and camping there. When Johnston's troops marched through Salt Lake City without breaking ranks, the Mormons began to move back to their homes, while the Army established what came to be known as Camp Floyd some forty miles southwest of Salt Lake in Cedar Valley. And so the bloodless "Utah War" ended with a negotiated compromise. A non-Mormon governor was installed and federal authority asserted, and the troops agreed to establish their post at a considerable distance from the major Mormon settlements.

9

These cabins located along the Black's Fork were built by the military.

Fort Bridger gets drafted!

When Johnston's Army and the accompanying civic officials left Camp Scott in June 1858 the Fort Bridger area lost most of its population; however, it still remained a very busy place. The post was promised new life when Colonel Johnston announced that a new Fort Bridger would be erected by part of his troops and the area would be converted into a military reservation. On 6 April 1859 President Buchanan supported Colonel Johnston's recommendation designating that a coal reservation of about a hundred acres located southwest of Fort Bridger be set aside for the use of the military. Then, following this action, he declared on July 14 that the military reservation of Fort Bridger should embrace territory twenty miles east and west, and twenty-five miles north and south, or about five hundred square miles. This was announced by Colonel Johnston in General Order #21, Department of Utah at Camp Floyd on 9 September 1859. Thus Fort Bridger became a military reservation with quite an extensive territory.

Unfortunately for the Mormons, the army did not take into consideration the fact that an agent for the Church had purchased the region from Jim Bridger and the federal government did not compensate the Mormons for their losses. Jim Bridger, ignoring his sale of the post to the Mormons, agreed to lease the property to the army for the sum of $600 a year for ten years with an option to purchase this land. If the army so desired at the end of ten years, it could purchase the property for the sum of $10,000. However, the army maintained that Bridger would have to prove that he actually had title to the area, and this he was unable to do.

Colonel Johnston designated Major William Hoffman of the Sixth United States Infantry to be commander of the post. Hoffman had made the difficult march from Fort Laramie to Fort Bridger bringing additional supplies during the early spring of 1858. Portions of the Sixth Infantry, the Tenth Infantry, and the First Calvalry were assigned to man the post. Taking advantage of this manpower, Hoffman proceeded to complete the storehouses and erect quarters for the troops. The soldiers brought timber down from the Uintah mountains and practically completed the construction of the post by the end of 1858. Some of this work was done under the direction of Lieutenant Colonel E. R. S. Canby of the Tenth Infantry who succeeded Major Hoffman as commander of Fort Bridger on 17 August 1858. Colonel A. G. Brackett, who was commander of Fort Bridger in 1870, left the following description of the post as he knew it.

The buildings that Major Hoffman directed to be built by the soldiers were described as log buildings neatly whitewashed. A creek, the middle branch of Black Fork, ran through the middle of the parade ground. There were ditches of pure water running in front and rear of the officers and men's quarters which made it pleasant enough. Trees had been planted in and about the fort and it looks like a beautiful village fairly embowered as one approaches it on the road from Carter's station 11 miles to the northward. I say it looks like a handsome village and so it is and handsome villages were by no means common in the summit on the Rocky Mountains. [1]

Colonel Canby continued to serve as the commanding officer of the post until 7 March 1860, when he left for Camp Floyd. He was replaced by Major R. C. Gatlin of the Seventh Infantry, who in turn was replaced on 4 June 1860 by Alfred Cumming of the Tenth. Two months later Cumming was replaced by Captain Franklin Gardner of the same regiment. These rapid changes in command at Fort Bridger reveal that the regular army was having problems because of the approaching war between the states.

Fort Bridger, of course, was visited periodically by people coming to Salt Lake Valley or going on to the coast. During 1859 a sizable number of Mormon immigrants including two hand-cart companies had passed by Fort Bridger, and in 1860 another hand-cart company came into Salt Lake Valley via this route. In addition to this there were some travelers, such as the famous English explorer and author, Sir Richard F. Burton, who was anxious to visit Salt Lake City primarily because of his interest in unique religious societies. He had a special interest in those with unusual sexual practices or attitudes, and he was anxious to investigate the Mormon practice of polygamy.

When Burton came into Fort Bridger in August of 1860 he wrote a

116

description of the fort, which was included in his *The City of the Saints*, published in 1862. The fort was 124 miles from Great Salt Lake City, but he wrote that the route "might be considerably shortened."

The garrison consisted of two companies of foot soldiers under the command of Captain F. Gardner of the 10th Regiment. The material of the house is pine and cedar brought from the Uinta hills whose black flank-supporting snow cones rise in the distance about 35 miles." [2]

He also confessed that when they arrived at Fort Bridger the first stop was to replenish the whiskey keg. He then called on the commanding officer, Captain Cumming, who introduced Burton's party to his officers and led them to his quarters where by means of "chat, solace tobacco and toddy which in these regions were necessary," they soon worked their way through the short three quarters of an hour they were allowed for an interview. Burton recorded that the "Officers complained very naturally of their isolation and their unpleasant duties which principally consist of keeping the roads open for, and the Indians from cutting off, parties of unmanageable immigrants who looked upon the Federal army as their humblest servants." [3] He also observed that the memory of the severe winter of 1857-58 was a "subject still sore to military ears." [4]

Pony Express

Early in 1860 a new development in continental communication began with the Majors, Russell, and Waddell freighting company's decision to establish a pony express across the Rockies and demonstrate that mail could be carried from St. Joseph, Missouri, to the Pacific Coast in eight days. In March 1860 the following advertisement was printed: [5]

To San Francisco in 8 days by the Central Overland California Pikes Peak Express Company. The first courier of the pony express will leave the Missouri River on Tuesday, April the 8th at 5:00 p.m. and will run regularly weekly thereafter, letter mail only. Point of departure on the Missouri River will be the telegraphic connection with the East which will be announced in due time. Telegraph messages from all parts of the country.

The pony express was a remarkable success in performance although it proved to be a financial failure. It operated from 3 April 1860 to 24 October 1861—less than nineteen months. Such a service during this early period of the Civil War was important however, bringing the far west and its treasures closer to the union. It also hastened the coming of the telegraph and the railroad. The pony express route ran between St. Joseph, Missouri, and Sacramento, California. From St. Joseph, Missouri to Fort Bridger the route followed much of the Oregon Trail, and from Fort Bridger the route led into Salt Lake City,

The pony express rider is the symbol of western courage and adventure.

southwest across the Salt Lake desert, through the Nevada deserts, and across the Sierra Nevadas into Sacramento.

In addition to serving as a major station for the pony express, Fort Bridger was also a main station for the freighting companies and the Overland mail. When Ben Holladay bought out the interest of Russell, Majors, and Waddell, and operated stagecoaches across the country, Fort Bridger became an important post along this route. In addition to this, Fort Bridger was also on the route of the Overland telegraph which was begun at the time the pony express was still in operation. Financed by the federal government, the Overland Telegraph Company from the east and the Pacific Telegraph Company from the west began erecting poles and stringing wires across the continent. After setting the first pole in July 1861, they raced to complete the task. The eastern section of the line passed Fort Bridger, and the crews working from the west coast met with the eastern line in Salt Lake City, thus joining the nation together by wire. Fort Bridger was an important junction point and relay station for the Overland telegraph.

Civil War Period

Captain Jesse A. Gove, Tenth Infantry, assumed command of Fort Bridger on 29 May 1861, remaining until August 9 of that year when the federal government withdrew almost all of their troops at the outbreak of the Civil War. Colonel Philip St. George Cooke of the Second Cavalry closed down Camp

118

These pony express buildings were constructed and preserved at the fort.

Floyd (then named Camp Chittenden) in Utah, and ordered that Fort Bridger sell most of its supplies at auction. Only a small force under Captain J. C. Clark, Fourth Artillery, stayed to man the post. Captain Gove gained his wish to be in the thick of the fight and was killed in the battle of Gaines Mill, Virginia, on 22 June 1862.

With the announcement of the supply auction at Fort Bridger, the Mormons, under the leadership of Lewis Robison, who had been the Mormon leader at Fort Bridger at the time of the withdrawal, once again began to assert their claims to the post. The government had never honored Robison's claims primarily because they did not honor Bridger's claim, and Robison had made his purchase of the fort from Bridger. But in 1861, with the withdrawal of the troops from Fort Bridger and the announcement of a public sale in July of that year, Lewis Robison wrote a letter to his friend, the commanding officer of the Mormon Militia, Daniel H. Wells, as follows:

Green River Territory
July 17, 1861

Dear Brother, I have just received notice of sale of public property at Fort Bridger which is to commence on the 26 of July. I expect to be at the sale. I have not learned whether they intend to sell the land improvements or not, but if so I suppose it would be well to enter a protest against such a sale. Should

119

there be anything sold that you want for yourself or public I wish you would inform me as soon as possible. Or any suggestions about the Bridger Ranch, or the property that might be left by the army. I suppose of course, it would be well for me to take possession if possible. I should have written to you before but had no time to attend.
(Signed) Your Brother, Lewis Robison.[6]

When Robison arrived at Fort Bridger, he posted a notice indicating that he intended to take possession of the fort if he could do so legally. At first informing all those who might be concerned that it was "... the intention of officers now in charge directing and commanding at Ft. Bridger to sell and transfer the same with improvements made thereon"; he then proceeded in the notice to outline his claim.

Now I therefore, Lewis Robison, the lawful and rightful owner of said premises and I hereby claim as my legal right the peaceful possession of the same together with all the buildings, corrals, yard fields, or improvements, whereon are pertances there belonging or in anywise pertaining and I do hereby forbid the sale of said premise or any portion thereof to any person or persons whatever, and I also warned all or any persons against purchasing, taking, or retaining possession of the same. Given under my hand and seal this 22nd day of July A. D. 1861, (Signed) Lewis Robison.[7]

Of course Robison's claim to ownership was not acceptable to Captain Gove and other military persons at the fort, and the sale went ahead as scheduled. However, there were a number of Mormons who came to the sale. After talking with Captain Gove, Robison was content to make a statement to the effect that "Capt. Gove was a gentlemen, but that the damn United States Government had robbed him of his property and he intended to have it."[8] One of the men who went from Salt Lake City to the sale was Hyrum B. Clawson, Brigham Young's son-in-law and business agent. He listed an interesting expense account for his trip to Fort Bridger, including in his list of purchases such things as glue pots, hair for horse collars, blankets, a teapot, corkscrews, one clock, one hundred feet of rope, candles and soap, etc.

After completion of the sale and Captain Gove's trip East with his troops to the Civil War, Captain J. C. Clark stayed with his small contingent only until December when he left Fort Bridger in the hands of a few privates and Sergeant Boger. With this removal of the official garrison and all commissioned officers, serious problems arose at Fort Bridger. The Shoshone Indians were hostile and there was special concern as to whether or not the Mormons would try to take advantage of the war situation and the removal of the troops to move in and reclaim the land that they thought was theirs. In this time of emergency a most unusual man emerged who was to dominate the history of Fort Bridger for many years, William A. Carter, who had come to Fort Bridger with Johnston's

Monument at Fort Bridger commemorating the pony express and Oregon trail.

121

Army as a sutler and post trader. He organized a volunteer army of mountain men from the surrounding country to protect the fort. He was also able to enlist the aid of Chief Washakie, sub-chief of the Shoshone Indians, who was the leader of the most reliable element of this tribe. This combination of mountaineers and Shoshone Indians under the leadership of the post trader kept the post in order until the coming of Colonel Patrick E. Conner and the California Volunteers.

Conner's Troops, recruits from California and Nevada, went to Salt Lake City to guard the overland mail and the telegraph line. Conner established his post on the hills above Salt Lake City and named it Camp Douglas in honor of Senator Stephen A. Douglas. He also sent a contingent east to Fort Bridger which, as a part of Utah territory, was also under his jurisdiction. In December 1862 Captain M. G. Lewis, who was with Company I, Third California Volunteers, arrived and assumed command of Fort Bridger. During the war years, Fort Bridger was garrisoned by companies of the Nevada and California Volunteers with various changes in command from time to time. Conner, in his report to the army commander-in-chief in December 1862 stated that he had assumed control of Fort Bridger, but felt that it was really not necessary to have troops there to quiet the apprehensions of the Overland Mail Company. Nevertheless, he agreed to obey the orders of the commanding general. Conner was very suspicious of the Mormons, reporting that they had made attacks on the telegraph lines or instigated attacks by the Indians on the telegraph stations in order to draw his forces away from Salt Lake City. He submitted no evidence for these assertions, however.

Little was done to maintain the post at Fort Bridger during the Civil War years. But during the late summer and fall of 1865, Major Noyes Baldwin of the First Nevada Volunteers, who served under General Patrick Conner in the Indian campaign of that year, was assigned to command the post. In addition to exploring the South Pass and the Wind River country, he built a road over the mountains from Fort Bridger to Brown's Hole on the Green River. After being mustered out of the service at Fort Douglas in July of 1866, he became an Indian trader and later a merchant in the South Pass and Lander region.

On 13 July 1866 after most of the volunteer troops of the Civil War had been mustered out, Captain Andrew S. Burt took command of the fort with companies F and H, First Battalion of the Eighteenth Infantry. An unnamed army officer left an interesting description of Fort Bridger as it appeared in 1866. He mentions that "... A tall stone wall with a parrallogram shape built by the Mormons for protection against the Indians still stands below the parade ground." Of the Black's Fork River, he praises the "... abundant supply of most delicious, clear, cool, water from the mountain springs." He continues:

The fort is located in an extensive basin surrounded by a succession of table-lands, rising one above the other which are styled benches. The benches are so

122

level and their slopes so regular that when observed from a distance they appear like an embankment for a railroad over a low flat country. . . . The spot appeared to be a very desireable one . . . were it not for its isolated position.

This spot was built by an officer nowhere better known or better appreciated for his sterling qualities than New Orleans, I refer to Gen. Canby. The quarters are constructed of hewn logs and those of the officers neatly plastered and provided with such conveniences as to afford them a comfortable home to those who have to occupy them.[9]

General James T. Rusling, who also visited the fort in 1866, gave the following description of its location and setting:

We halted at Fort Bridger two or three days, to inspect this post and consider its bearings, and so became pretty well rested up again. Some miles below the Fort, Green River subdivides into Black's and Smith's Forks, and the valleys of both of these we found contained much excellent land. . . . The post itself is 7,000 feet above the sea, and the Wahsatch Mountains just beyond were reported snow-capped the year round. Black's Fork runs directly through the parade ground, in front of the officers' quarters, and was said to furnish superb trout fishing in season. In summer, it seemed to us, Bridger must be a delightful place; but in the winter, rather wild and desolate.[10]

In the summer of 1867, the discovery of gold near the source of the Sweetwater River brought new burdens and excitement into the life of Fort Bridger. Throngs of gold seekers and adventurers from Salt Lake City, Montana, and California, rushed to the new gold fields in such numbers that South Pass City was laid out in October 1867 on Willow Creek; and, of course, those coming from California and Salt Lake City made Fort Bridger their chief base of supplies before moving into the Sweetwater Region. By this time, Major Burt had been succeeded by Captain Anson Mills, who remained until August 1867.

In 1866 Wells-Fargo, a freighting company that had bought out Ben Holladay, made Fort Bridger one of its main stations, and it remained prominent until the coming of the railroad in 1869.

Wyoming was established as a territory on 25 July 1868 embracing that portion of Utah territory in which Fort Bridger was situated. This brought an end to Fort Bridger's eighteen-year official connection with the territory of Utah.

One note of interest before leaving this particular period of Fort Bridger's history is that Fort Bridger published Wyoming's first newspaper. It was published as the Daily Telegraph. Only one copy has survived—the eighth number of the first volume dated Fort Bridger, Utah Territory, 26 June 1863. H. Brundige, who was listed as proprietor, was undoubtedly the printer as well. This diminutive frontier newspaper was printed on one side only, a sheet 6½ by

123

Patrick Conner and his men controlled Fort Bridger during the Civil War.

124

Panoramic view of Fort Bridger after several years of military occupancy.

10½ inches. Terms of the subscription were listed at $1 for one month, $10 for the year. At the bottom of the second column was the inevitable printers' advertisement, "Job work of all kinds done at this office." How long Brundige's newspaper continued business publication is not known, but he must be credited with being the first printer in Wyoming.

Coming of the Union Pacific

At the same time as the publication of the newspaper, another important project was to have a serious impact on the history of Fort Bridger—the building of the transcontinental railroad by the Union Pacific Company. Engineers, surveyors, and detachments of employees guarding the overland stage route stayed at Fort Bridger. Troops were employed in erecting an additional storehouse and repairing old ones under Major J. H. Bellstar, post quartermaster. During 1868-69, while the railroad was under construction, portions of the garrison at Bridger comprising B, C, F, and H Companies of the Thirty-sixth Infantry under command of Lieutenant Colonel H. A. Morrow were constantly engaged in escorting engineering parties of the railroad and in guarding the overland stage route. The railroad route by-passed Fort Bridger nine miles north, resulting in the establishment of Carter Station at the junction of the railroad and the new road built from Fort Bridger. The railroad provided transportation across the continent on a new route and ended the role Fort

Bridger had played in the westward migration. The railroad "made Wyoming"—which is rather ironic, since it heralded the decline of Fort Bridger, which had just been transferred to Wyoming from Utah.

Various Activities After 1869

The military reservation at Fort Bridger was reduced to four miles square pursuant to an order from the War Department issued December 1869. This reduction order was revoked in October 1870, but once again, on 25 March 1871, the War Department reduced Fort Bridger reservation to four square miles for military purposes and turned over 196 square miles to the Interior Department. An executive order was issued 22 May 1871 reserving an additional area for the fort cemetery established in 1866. During the period following 1869 the post had been garrisoned by companies of the Thirty-sixth Infantry. Additional storehouses and quarters were built at this time and old ones were repaired under the direction of John H. Belcher, the post quartermaster.

While the military importance of Fort Bridger continued to wane, it became the center of other important activities during the summer of 1870. For example, it served as a base for a scientific expedition sponsored by Yale University. The party, composed of students and graduates of the university under the direction of O. C. March, engaged in examining the fossil beds near Fort Bridger in 1871. An article in *Harpers Magazine* mentions the great assistance given the party by Major Mott and Judge Carter, but did not attempt to report the geological results of the expedition.

In the fall of the same year, 1870, a geological survey of the Uinta Mountains was made by Dr. Ed B. Hayden, the U.S. Geologist. He used Fort Bridger as a base of operations and in his report wrote of his deep gratitude to the military personnel who cooperated with him.

I have already spoken of my obligations to Judge Carter to whom I was indebted for many favors and much valuable information. To him this portion of the west has been in the past and will be in the future more indebted for his prosperity and development than all others. I take pleasure here in adding to the testimony of the fidelity and truthfulness of his statements in regard to its resources.[11]

In June 1871 Brigadier General C. C. Auger, commanding the Department of the Platte, ordered Captain W. A. Jones of the Corps of Engineers to make a scientific reconnaissance in Wyoming, including the region around Fort Bridger. The party arrived in June 1871 and used the post as its principal headquarters. They fixed the boundaries of the reservation, and turned over 484 square miles to the Interior Department in February of 1872. Despite the decline of the post, new barracks buildings and a new small frame building for the laundresses' quarters were erected at the fort. The post commander at this time, Colonel Albert C. Brackett, Second Cavalry, wrote a most interesting history and description of Fort Bridger, and Brigadier General William H. Bisbee related his experience at Fort Bridger during this time as follows:

As I knew Bridger proper 50 years ago, that is 1874-75, it was occupied by Hd. Qtrs. and four companies of the 4th U.S. Infantry. All buildings were made of logs, single story, all located around the square with a parade ground in the center. Conventional form of defensive building in early Indian days but it was in no other sense a fort. Black's Fork ran through the parade grounds south to north. There were within the main garrison limits 20 buildings, eight officers quarters, four barracks for soldiers, 2 quartermaster and commissary storehouses. One hospital, one guardhouse, one bakery, one stable, one recreation hall and the trading store and the residence of Judge W. A. Carter. As more ancient history items I do not recall buildings that might have been termed a fort and defense place except the old cobblestone wall and the building in the S[outh] W[est] corner of the square [which] was used as a storehouse.

The Post and public cemetary was on a sagebrush plateau one mile south on the right bank of Black's Fork and overlooking it. Nearby on Smith's Fork are Fossil grounds where the friends from the Yale University and Prof. Marsh and students and others found valuable specimens, one a massive Mastadon which they named "Uintatherium." Yale museum may have reserved some of these collections.

Bridger was an annual meetingplace for Chief Washakee and the Shoshones from the Wind River in the North with the Utes from the White River, South. Cattle belonging to Judge Carter and a few other ranchers on Smith's and Henry's Fork were in small groups scattered among the hills towards the mountains. [12]

Soon after the establishment of Carter's station, a railroad station for supplies situated nine to ten miles to the north, Fort Bridger was almost completely discontinued as a military garrison. However, in 1879 General Crook sent Bisbee from Fort Fred Steel with two companies of infantry to reoccupy it and later to construct a wagon trail from it over the Uinta Mountains to the newly established Fort Thornberg, named for Major T. T. Thornberg of the Fourth Infantry, who had been killed the previous September by the Indians on Milk River. The work, all by soldier labor, progressed as well as could be expected for a limited force of men without machinery. The corduroy passageway through the marshy sections high in the range proved fairly adequate, though not ideal for heavily loaded wagons. It was discontinued by General Howard after General Crook had gone back to Arizona.

Upon the completion of the Rio Grande Western Railroad in 1883, and by a change in location of Fort Thornberg, shorter routes for transporting supplies were secured, and Fort Bridger's usefulness for military purposes ended. In 1883, however, the garrisons of Companies B, C, and G, and the Ninth Infantry under the direction of Lieutenant Colonel Thomas M. Anderson erected some

127

Sir Richard Burton, famous British adventurer, described life at the fort.

additional barracks and quarters there. From November 1883 to December 1885, Company H, Fifteenth Infantry under F. E. Eltonhead, worked on the telegraph line from Fort Bridger to Carter Station, substituting iron poles for the old wooden ones.

Another act of Congress approved on 7 July 1884 disposed of useless military reservations. The coal reservation of nearly one hundred acres was turned over to the Interior Department by the War Department. Fort Bridger's usefulness seemed to be over. But even through this activity there was some increase of the garrison in August 1884. Lt. Col. Anderson, relieved from command by Lt. Col. Alexander Chambers of the Twenty-first Infantry, compiled much of the information concerning the military occupancy of the post, based on the records of Mr. Herbert Howe Bancroft, a famous western historian.

In November 1884 an active inspector general recommended the abandonment of the fort because "of the great altitude, no gardens could be made, frost every month, winters long and severe, no summer other than a few pleasant weeks in July and August, expensive to keep up, no military reason for existence." No information is at hand from after the period covered by Col. Chambers's report of 4 January 1885 until the post was finally abandoned in 1890. The War Department files report that in June 1889, however, a complete water system was laid throughout the post, although not long afterward on 10 April 1890 an order directed the withdrawal of troops from a number of forts west of the Mississippi including Fort Bridger. October 1, 1890 was the date set for its abandonment. On October 14, the War Department formally transferred the Bridger military reservation to the Interior Department. The area was described as being 16 square miles, 10,240 acres. Some of the troops left the post September 15, some October 1, and finally a small detachment of the Seventeenth Infantry left on 6 November 1890, on which day Fort Bridger ceased to be a military post. It seems somewhat ironic that with the recommendation that the post be abandoned, the government would develop a new water system there. Perhaps the military could supply some rational explanation for such action. In any case, the military period of Fort Bridger's history was officially ended in 1890.

10

Chief Washakie posing with his people for early photographer W. H. Jackson.

Fort Bridger's role in Indian relations

One of the most important activities at Fort Bridger during the military period was the attempt of the federal government to keep peace with and give aid to the Indians of the region. As a rule such activities were supervised by civilian superintendents of Indian affairs, but such men were dependent on the cooperation of the army, and often Army officers served as sub-agents.

Jacob Forney, who came west with Johnston's Army, was superintendent of Indian affairs during the difficult winter of 1857-58 and continued to serve with Fort Bridger as his headquarters until he moved to Salt Lake City in 1859. After describing the difficulties he encountered in reaching Camp Scott, he made his first report concerning the Indians of the region.

The tribes and the fragments of tribes with whom I had business relations during my forced residence at Camp Scott were as follows: to wit- on the 2nd day of December last, I visited San Pitch, principal chief of the Utahs and a few of his men. They wished to see Agent Hurt who was then residing at Camp Scott. I gave them a few presents and this was my first official act with the Indians. On the 10th of December, Little Soldier, Chief and Benjamin Simons, sub-chief of a band of Shoshones and some of their principal men called on me. Several merchants however, who had recently and for several years resided in Salt Lake City and who were well acquainted with this tribe from their proximity in the Mormon settlements regarded the visit with suspicion. I learned, however, that their reason for visiting camp was to ascertain the object and ultimate destination of so many soldiers in the territory. All this was explained to them and after receiving some presents they departed for their homes in Weber Valley. Ben Simons understands and speaks English sufficiently well to act as interpreter. I visited this tribe in April 1858 when they were then encamped on the Bear River. There is no tribe of Indians in the territory with whom I have any acquaintances that have been so much discommoded by the introduction of white population as the Shoshones. For the past few years they have been compelled to live in the mountains as the game has been driven off the lowlands where the snow frequently falls to such depths as to be a disadvantage to man and beast. Not withstanding all the disadvantages under which they labor from the introduction of the white populace I cannot learn that they have ever molested our citizens but on the contrary have always been friendly. [1]

Forney continued to send out reports from Fort Bridger concerning the Indian tribes of the region and it became apparent that the post was going to become a center for Indian affairs of that particular area. In a letter from Fort Bridger dated 21 May 1858 Superintendent Forney reported to the acting commissioner of Indian affairs that he had succeeded in consummating a treaty of peace between the Snake tribe [Shoshone] under Chief Washakie and his five sub-chiefs and the Ute Tribe under White Eye Sow and Sand Pitch, equal chiefs. These two tribes had been at enmity for years, fighting and killing each other and endangering the lives and property of the whites. "I've seen and talked with both tribes before they met here and at my request they met in council in my office. All differences were adjusted and I have good reason to believe that the peace will be permanent," was his optimistic report. A line dividing these Indians had never been explained to them, but now they understood where the dividing line was located. After telling of the treaty and visiting the tribes Forney made a statement concerning his expenditures for so many presents to the Indians. He felt they had been ". . . faithful to the government and never molested any of our people." He added that

Three of the tribes have never received any presents. These Indians were and are in a position which if exposed could have done us more harm than the Mormons. After consulting a few friends last fall and the destitute condition of the Indians, many really almost naked and starving, I felt it to be my duty to do as I have done. I have given all the presents I intend to give to the Indians in this portion of the territory which at the price even here will not exceed $8,000 to the end of the fiscal year. [2]

Forney moved to Salt Lake Valley in 1859 and reported that most of the tribes were either Shoshone—Snake, as they were known—or Ute. The only exception was a small tribe of Bannocks numbering about five hundred. Horn,

132

the principal chief of the Bannocks, visited Fort Bridger in April 1858 where Forney had an interview with him. This chief claimed a home for himself and his people in the territory and informed Forney that the old men around him had been children in this particular country. Bridger, Forney's interpreter at the time, said that he had traded with this tribe in that section of the country for the last thirty years and that when he had first known them they had numbered 1,200 lodges. Forney granted the Bannocks a home in the region with the consent of Washakie and his Shoshones. The two tribes intermarried extensively and lived together, according to Bridger.

The Indians mentioned most often in conjunction with Fort Bridger were the Shoshone under Chief Washakie. This tribe seemed to make their headquarters between Fort Bridger and the Rockies and occasionally went east of Bridger for the elk hunt.

The year 1862 was a critical year along the Overland Trail. Immigrant travel by the familiar South Pass route became hazardous and the Overland mail route was shifted south to the old Cherokee trail between Denver and Fort Bridger. The U.S. Government, which had taken Shoshone friendship for granted, all at once awakened to the value and meaning of friendship and even began to suggest a treaty. Part of the reason for this attitude was the report that Indians had destroyed mail stations between Fort Bridger and the North Platte, burning the coaches and mail bags and killing the drivers. Reacting, Adjutant General Thomas Washington called upon Mormon Church President Brigham Young for a company of cavalry to protect the mail route. It seems a little strange that he should call on ex-governor Young when his own appointed governor was there, but he apparently felt that Young would be able to furnish troops immediately and he was right. Four companies of mounted men were made part of the United States Army to guard the Overland mail and Overland telegraph in and around the area of Fort Bridger for a few months during the Civil War. In August 1862 Brigadier General James Craig reported that he had sent the Utah troops to Bridger to guard the line from that post to Salt Lake City, which left him with only his original contingent to protect the four hundred miles intervening between Laramie and Fort Bridger. Indian agent Luther Mann, who had come to Fort Bridger in 1861, reported that "brutal murders" had been committed by the Shoshone and Bannock Indians. He added that although he was glad to report Washakie and his band were innocent of "any acts of violence or theft," talks with Washakie made him apprehensive

. . . that a general outbreak of hostilities will take place throughout the entire region and country. Large herds of stock have been stolen and driven off by predatory bands of Shoshones during the present season. I would most earnestly recommend that three or four companies of soldiers be stationed at Fort Bridger. It's capacity being ample without expenditure of a very small means to quarter that number.[3]

He asserted in a report on August 13 that a robbery of two hundred head of stock owned by Jack Robinson and other settlers took place near Fort Bridger within six miles of the camp of the men Brigham Young had sent up to protect the Overland Trail.

General Conner, whose soldiers replaced the Mormon companies in 1862, believed in using military force to curb the Indian depredations. Apparently his policy was effective in some cases as at one time almost 900 Snake Indians "signified a desire to be friendly" by returning to General Connor 150 horses and mules stolen from the whites. The Shoshones "begged of General Connor to be allowed to go back to Washakie's band, and Pocatello also begged for peace." [4]

Conner continued his brutal policy in January 1863 when he led his forces against an almost defenseless band of Shoshone Indians in what became known as the Battle of Bear River near present-day Preston, Idaho. As estimated three to four hundred Indians were killed by Conner's troops.

Peace Treaties
One of the highlights of Indian relations developed in 1863 when on June 20 Luther Mann, the Indian agent, was able to conclude a treaty with the Shoshones. He telegraphed Washington saying:

Sir, 500 Shoshone or Snake Indians will visit this agency today for the purpose of delivering up stolen stock in their possession and pledging themselves to keep quiet in the future. They are entirely destitute of food and clothing. Shall I feed them now for a few days? Please answer immediately. Superintendent Doty being now north I am compelled to apply for instructions from you direct. [5]

He received instructions to feed the Indians and was happy to conclude a treaty with them which he reported as follows: "Articles of Agreement made at Fort Bridger in Utah Territory this second day of July, one thousand eight hundred and sixty-three between the United States of America represented by his commissioners and the Shoshone nation of Indians represented by its chief, principal men and warriors of the eastern bands." [6] Consisting of six articles, the treaty declared a firm and perpetual peace and friendship between the Shoshone nation and the United States.

It also promised that the routes used by white men and the government of the United States would be safe and without molestation by the Shoshone. This included agricultural settlements and military posts along the route. Ferries could be maintained over the rivers, and telegraph lines and overland stage traffic would be protected along the route. Boundaries were spelled out. *Article V* indicated that the United States was aware of the inconvenience caused by the destruction of game along the route traveled by the whites and

134

by the formation of agricultural and mining settlements, and was willing to fairly compensate the Indians for this loss. Estimating the loss and inconvenience, the United States promised to pay the bands of the Shoshone nation who signed the treaty the sum of $10,000 annually for a term of twenty years. The Shoshone nation acknowledged the receipt of such annuities as a full compensation equivalent to loss of game and the rights and privileges hereby conceded. The commissioners gave them provisions and clothing amounting to $6,000 as presents at the conclusion of this treaty. It was finally signed by Washakie and other chiefs at Fort Bridger, on 2 July 1863 in the presence of Jack Robinson, interpreter, and James Duane Doty and Luther Mann, Jr., commissioners.

It was estimated that those chiefs who agreed to the pact represented between 3,000 and 4,000 Indians, 1,000 of which were present at the conclusion of the treaty. It must have had some positive impact on the Indians, because a report by Major Gallagher to General Conner in the spring of 1864 said, "I have the honor to report to the general commanding officer that one of Washakie's Indians named Woe-on-grant brought to this post yesterday nineteen horses which had been stolen and delivered them into my hands." He made the following statement:

He said, that being out hunting in the Wind River Mountains he came to four lodges of Indians and they are a branch of the Snake tribe called Shoshone or sheep eaters. They informed him that they had stolen 24 horses from white men who were mining or prospecting near the Beaverhead. This Indian said he told them that a treaty had been made with the Indians last summer which was the first information they had had of it. They delivered to him twenty horses, three having got away from him and he brought them to Fort Bridger. One of the horses was kept by Washakie's Indians which I think I can get, he said. 19 horses are here which I shall keep until I know the wishes of the general in regard to them.[7]

A year later, in September 1865, Luther Mann was able to report that Washakie's group of Shoshones was still very peaceful and friendly. He estimated their number to be around 1,800 men, women, and children. He said that they were friendly with the Bannocks to the north and the Utes to the south, but were hostile to the tribes on the eastern boundaries, such as the Sioux, Arapahoes, Cheyenne, and Crows. Washakie, he reported, "feels himself too weak to engage himself in any aggressive movements against these eastern tribes but says if he should be attacked, he would give them battle."[8] When this tribe arrived at Fort Bridger in June of 1865, hearing of General Conner's expedition against the Sioux, they presented themselves armed and equipped, eager to join the troops in the campaign against their old foes. Only the lack of suitable military organization moving from this point prevented the

This rare photo at the fort shows Washakie (left) with dancing Shoshones.

acceptance of their services. Mann reported giving the government subsidy to Washakie and said, "It affords me pleasure in stating the Indians belonging to the district are peaceful and well disposed and in all of their acts they have been in strict accordance with friendly relations which heretofore existed between themselves and the white resident population of this territory." [9]

Luther Mann's report in 1866 was similar in describing peaceful relations with the Indians in and around Fort Bridger and especially, of course, with Washakie. In July 1866 a post ultimately named for Washakie was established near the present site of Lander, Wyoming. At first named for Brigadier General C. C. Auger of the United States Army, it was subsequently named after Frederick H. Brown who was killed at the Fort Kearney massacre in December 1866. Finally, in December 1878, the name of the post was changed to Fort Washakie in honor of the illustrious chief of the Shoshone.

In September 1868 Agent Mann reported that Chief Washakie retained the same upright and manly character that he had ever sustained from the first settlement of Utah. His control over the Indians was more absolute than any other chief within the superintendency, and such influence was uniformly exercised wisely and to the best interest of all the Indians. In a full and well-considered report, agent Mann transmitted a detailed account of the successful conference between General Auger and the eastern Shoshone and

136

Bannocks. Setting apart a portion of the Wind River Valley as a reservation for eastern Shoshone was calculated to perpetuate the good feeling that had existed between them and the whites. On 3 July 1868 at Fort Bridger, representatives of the government headed by General William T. Sherman signed the treaty. Washakie and several sub-chiefs represented the Indians. The treaty was subsequently ratified by the Senate and on 21 February 1869 was proclaimed by President Johnson. This proclamation established the duration of the treaty and contained the signatures of the government officials and the Indians.

The language of the treaty seemed to indicate that no earlier treaty had been entered into by the government and these tribes. Among other provisions, it set aside and established a reservation for the Shoshone which included, in a general way, the Wind River country. Boundaries were not very definitely fixed and referred mainly to watersheds and streams.

The treaty provided that the Indians should make their permanent home within the reservation and the whites should be excluded therefrom except the Indian agent to be appointed as necessary and other officers and employees of the government. Among such were named a physician, a schoolteacher, a farmer, a carpenter, a blacksmith, a surveyor, and a miller. Provision was made for the government to build lumber and grist mills, a residence and office for the agent, a schoolhouse, and residences for several employees above named. There was also a provision for building an additional schoolhouse and supplying an additional teacher for every thirty additional children between the ages of six and sixteen who could be persuaded to attend school. [10]

The government clearly contemplated an effort on its part to educate and civilize the Indians and Washakie looked with favor upon this purpose. Washakie was described by P. L. Williams, an attorney residing in Salt Lake City: "Washakie could not speak nor understand English and in his association with white men he was invariably accompanied by Norcock, his interpreter, who was a very intelligent young man who spoke and understood English very well. . . . Washakie, at this time, was about 60 years of age." He was described as being a "broad shouldered, deep chested, muscular man and had been in his young manhood no doubt possessed of great physical strength and endurance. Stories of remarkable feats of his nature were tradition among his tribesmen. His hair was slightly sprinkled with grey. His face was free from wrinkles, expression was kindly but always serious and thoughtful." [11]

The treaty created the Wind River Reservation, centering it in and around Fort Washakie where the Shoshone Indians still reside. The Bannock Indians were moved to Fort Hall in 1871. This was the last important treaty made with the Shoshone Indians in Wyoming who ceded to the government all of Wyoming west of the North Platte River and south of the Wind River Mountains, extending northward to the old Blackfoot boundary in Yellowstone National Park. According to Bartlette's *History of Wyoming*, this section included the counties of Uintah, Sweetwater, Lincoln except a little of the northeast corner, and part of Cardon west of the North Platte River.

Fort Bridger continued to be a center for work among the Shoshone, Bannock, and Ute Indians during the 1870s and 1880s. For example, in a dispatch dated Fort Bridger, Wyoming, 6 October 1870, agent J. W. Wham wrote that when he arrived at Fort Bridger in August of 1870 he found that a portion of the treaty requiring an office to be open at all times for the purpose of hearing complaints and attending to other business for these Indians had been entirely ignored and neglected. Since the making of the treaty on 3 July 1868 no office had been kept open. "How is it possible," he wrote, "to expect a tribe of Indians to live up to their agreement when the government neglects to carry into effect the first principal of its treaty stipulations." He went on:

The agency is not established nor the buildings erected as provided by the treaty of July 3, 1868. These Indians were off on a hunt when I arrived and have not yet returned, however, I have learned from Maj. D. G. Gordon that he had met Washakee and his tribe and that he was well disposed but sent word to a new agent to get some beef and flour that he wanted something for his people to eat. These Indians desire to commence farming but how is that possible when not an ounce of subsistance is provided for their first years support. An Indian lives by hunting and he does nothing more to supply his wants. If he farms he cannot hunt, if he does not hunt, he starves and hence the necessity of supplying him with beef and flour for the first year.[12]

This is an example of the pattern that the United States followed throughout the history of its relations with the Indians. Treaties were made only to be broken. Some corrupt individuals failed to carry out their assignments. Others, sincere men like Wham, attempted to do the best they could to carry out the terms of the treaty. Captain J. Patterson, who was U.S. agent for the Shoshone and Bannock Indians, submitted his report to the governor, J. A. Campbell, who in turn sent it to the Washington agency. He reported difficulty with the Sioux Indians who reportedly had violated terms of their treaty. He felt the best answer to the problems lay in the policies already outlined—that the Indians "should be compelled to go on their reservation and stay on it." He felt that as soon as enough funds were appropriated to sustain them, it would be easier to induce the Shoshones and Bannocks to settle on their reservations. A band of Northern Arapahoes had already seemed willing to make peace with the Shoshones. He hoped the Indians would engage in cultivation and learn from the whites. He included a statement that he felt the reservations should not be too "great in extent."

A small reservation containing a sufficiency of tillable land and furnished employment, and subsistance for all the Indians on it is better than a large tract of land with limits which can never be thoroughly understood and over the

138

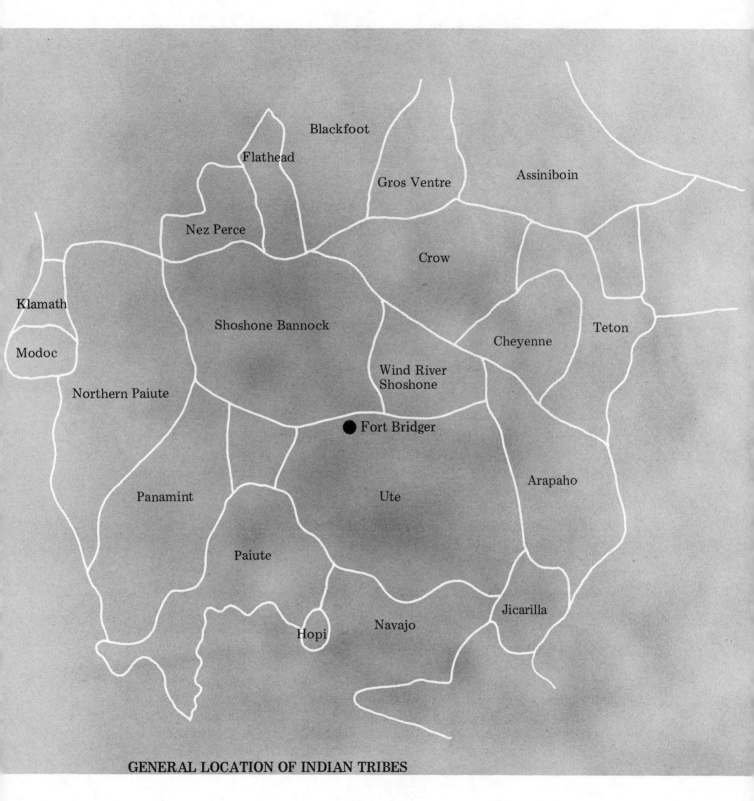

GENERAL LOCATION OF INDIAN TRIBES

Washakie, or "Shoot the Buffalo Running," photographed by W. H. Jackson.

extent it is impossible for an agent to exercise supervision. My opinion is that these Indian reservations should be located as far from White settlements as possible thus removing the temptations of encroaching on the lands of the Indians and at the same time remove the Indians from the bad influence of the evil designing men who at all times were ready to take advantage of their ignorance and vicious inclinations. [13]

In July 1870 Lieutenant George G. W. Flemming, who was designated as agent for the Bannock and Shoshone Indians, reported from Fort Bridger concerning difficulty with the Arapahoes. He said at first the Shoshones would not hold any intercourse with the Arapahoes. Washakie said that the Arapahoes would not accept any treaties but would soon violate any treaty. He also charged them with having killed the people in that valley and the Sweetwater mines the previous summer. Although the Arapahoes acknowledged this they said that they wanted peace. After a great deal of talk Flemming succeeded in getting the Shoshones and Arapahoes to make a treaty between themselves and remain at peace until the government could be heard from. The Arapahoes made many demands and finally declared that they were dissatisfied with the

140

provisions they had received. In March, Flemming purchased sugar, tobacco, bacon, and coffee for them, and a few blankets for the chief. About the same time, Flemming reported that he heard the Arapahoes were obtaining ammunition. Immediately he applied to the post at Fort Bridger for military aid. However, he was refused. He then reported that the Arapahoes had attacked and had killed several persons near Atlantic and Miners Delight and that a body of citizens described as mainly thieves and cutthroats had retaliated. The citizens' group had marched in the vicinity of Camp Auger and brutally murdered eleven unarmed old men and women including Black Bear, one of their chiefs.

Washakie of the Shoshones was fearful of these hostile Indians. He was also doubtful he would be able to get his tribe to begin farming until the government provided some farm implements with which they could start to work. The old chief seemed very anxious to have the Bannocks—numbering about one thousand to fifteen hundred—join his reservation since a large number of Bannocks and Shoshones had intermarried. Lieutenant Flemming also reported that he had found Washakie hunting on various forks of the Green River and Bear River. He finally brought the chief to Carter Station on the Union Pacific Railroad on May 31, where he and his tribe remained until joined by others totalling some sixty-four lodges. They camped about thirteen miles west of Fort Bridger. Flemming reported that he had issued them flour and beef. He had also employed a physician, who succeeded in vaccinating a few of them although many of them required more time to think about being vaccinated. A great deal of sickness among them had resulted in seven deaths since their departure from the Wind River Valley. They insisted their agency was still at Bridger until the promised buildings were erected and farm implements were furnished for them to work with.

One year later James Irwin, U.S. Indian agent, reported that the situation had improved. He indicated that part of the treaty made at Bridger in July 1868 was being carried out. However, he felt they should still try to honor the promise that they would keep an office open and distribute annuities at Fort Bridger. He was able to report that on the Wind River Reservation buildings were being commenced: dwelling houses for the agent and extra employees, storehouses, a mission or schoolhouse, a small fort stockade, and a smithshop. He also reported that twelve acres of ground had been plowed and fenced and a fair crop raised that year. He described the Wind River Reservation as beautifully located in a highly productive though rather narrow valley only three miles wide and twenty-five to thirty miles long, with a good climate. Irwin felt that the selection was a very good one. He also reported that it was difficult to get the Bannocks to settle down, as they were scattered over several territories and hardly knew what reservation they belonged to. He felt that a treaty would have to be made for them to keep them away from the Sweetwater mines, as it would then be impossible to observe the treaty in regard to white men encroaching upon their reservation. In conclusion, he stated that the Indians were

Another W. H. Jackson photo shows three women with a child on a cradle board.

"yet in a wild state having learned from their intercourse with the whites little more than their vices. Yet from their present peaceful attitude there seems to be no reason that with good management, work satisfactory to the government and gratifying to the friends of humanity can be accomplished at this agency."[14]

Reports continued to be much the same as in past years. One report by Flemming indicated that the Bannocks had never really occupied the Wind River Reservation except for a few months of 1871 and the spring of 1872 when about four hundred of them were present at the agency. They could not agree, being very mean and suspicious toward each other. So the Bannocks were allowed to withdraw to the Portneuf country near the Kamas prairies located in Idaho Territory. They were secured in their rights and privileges in that country by provisions of the same treaty, and came to be known as the Fort Hall Bannocks. Concluding his report, Flemming wrote:

From that time until the present, the Shoshones have enjoyed themselves alone except for roaming bands of Western Shoshones, Bannocks, Crows, White River Utes, and Uinta Valley Utes. . . . Recently, however, the Northern Arapahoes had been transferred to this agency. From this time forward, therefore, the Shoshones and Arapahoes will be identified with whatever pertains to the future history of this reservation and although still called the Shoshone and Bannock Agency, in Wyoming, not a Bannock in the United States has any rights except the few that have been legally incorporated into the Shoshones. . . .[15]

By the time Fort Bridger was abandoned by the government, the problems concerning the Indians had been reasonably well solved. The various Indian reservations at Wind River, Fort Hall, and in the Uinta Basin area took care of them. It was no longer necessary to have military detachments at Fort Bridger to keep peace among the Indians.

11

This sign stands where Judge Carter's home stood before it was burned.

William Alexander Carter – "Mr. Fort Bridger"

Although Jim Bridger founded the famous fort and gave it his name, he actually spent very little time at his establishment, having relatively little to do with its growth and development. A very different sort of man came to Fort Bridger with Johnston's Army in 1857 and became the dominant force at Bridger for twenty-four years until his untimely death in 1881. This man, William Alexander Carter, came west as a sutler with the army at the behest of his good friend General William S. Harney, but he expanded his activities to become a merchant, rancher, justice of the peace, and probate judge. He was also a friend and peacemaker with the Indians, and a genial host to the visitors and army personnel at Fort Bridger. His home was a center of culture and refinement, including an impressive library and a Steinway piano. When the post was abandoned, Carter's widow gained the title to the post and his descendants have retained an interest and exerted an important influence in the development of the fort into a state museum.

Having been born and raised in Virginia, Judge Carter developed and always retained the character and charm of a Southern gentleman, despite his years of rousting about with the army. He had enlisted at an early age and served in the Seminole Indian War, where he became friends with General Harney. After his discharge, he remained with the army as a sutler or purveyor, and it was in this capacity that he came to Fort Bridger.

Carter became especially prominent at the fort when it was practically abandoned by the army during the Civil War. He organized the mountain men

145

into a local militia and enlisted the aid of Chief Washakie to help him defend the fort against hostile Indians. He was relieved of this duty when Col. Patrick Conner and his California volunteers took over command in 1862. Conner was suspicious of Carter, feeling that he was taking advantage of his position to enrich himself at the expense of the U.S. Government. There was no doubt that he was becoming rich, but Conner's suspicions of some illegal activity seem unjustified. Almost everyone who became acquainted with Carter remarked about his generosity, courtliness, and warm hospitality.

One of the first to record his impressions of Carter's operations at the fort was the famous British soldier of fortune, adventurer, and writer, Richard Burton. Burton reported that his party was "conducted by Judge Carter to a building which combined the function of post office and sutler's store, the judge being also sutler, and performing both parts, I believe, to the satisfaction of everyone."[1]

One army officer who came to Fort Bridger at this time said that as they approached the fort and conversed with individuals who could give information about the post he usually heard such a remark as the following: "And you will find Judge Carter the sutler there, a finer gentleman you'll never meet. We met the judge and he proved to be all that had been represented." The officer continued:

We found him to be a high toned and intelligent and hospitable Virginia gentlemen. Universally popular with all who associated with him. And deservedly so. His store contains a larger assortment of every variety of goods and wares than any other establishment West of the Mississippi River. I was informed by good authority that his interests in the East last year, this was 1865, amounted to in excess of $180,000.00. This large trade is by no means confined to those at the post but principally with the miners and immigrants. His success in business had doubtless surpassed his expectations. I have seldom met a more hospitable gentleman than Judge Carter and there is always a place at his table for a visitor at the post or a passing friend. The pleasure of entertaining a guest is the only remuneration he will receive for his liberality.[2]

Another visitor at the fort in 1866 was Brevet Brigadier General James T. Rusling, inspector, quartermaster's department, who arrived there on an official trip in October. In his book entitled *Across America*, published in 1874, General Rusling described the fort:

. . . Apart from the garrison, the only white people there, or near there, were Judge Carter and his employees. A few lodges of Shoshones, the famous Jim Bridger with them, were encamped below the Fort; but they were quiet and peaceable. The Government Reservation there embraced all the best land for many miles and practically excluded settlements; otherwise no doubt quite a population would soon spring up.[3]

146

He also described Judge Carter and the success of his store and his farming.

Judge Carter, the sutler and postmaster at Bridger, and a striking character in many ways, already had several large tracts under cultivation, by way of experiment, and the next year he expected to try more. His grass was magnificant; his oats, barley, and potatoes, very fair; but his wheat and Indian corn wanted more sunshine.

His store grew as a trade store with the Indians and emigrants, and in 1866 he reported his sales at $100,000 per year.

In 1867, Mr. A. K. McClure, a stage traveler who visited the Fort, described Judge Carter's operation as follows:

We were met at the station by Judge Carter and made to share his proverbial hospitality. I had met him at Denver when we were all blockaded there and was glad to be welcomed to the abode of civilization after a week of unpleasant adventure among Indian and Ranchman. He had a comfortable house, an estimable wife, several daughters (most of them East at school), a fine piano, and library and everything that is to be found in residences. He is Virginian by birth, tall, spare, flaxen-haired, gentleman, with light flowing beard and mustache. Evidently a gentleman of much more that ordinary culture and character. He has expended some $40,000 dollars in building on the military land and has an immense store. He deals largely with friendly Indians and immigrants and supplies the garrison with sutlers stores. And as usual in his exercise of Western hospitality he took us to his well filled cellar and I declined Whiskey, Brandy, Gin, Rum, and so on he went right on to something else until he turned up a bottle of what he called "favorite bitters" and that, he said, I must drink. Being under military rule, I, of course, complied. Before I had the glass empty he had a bottle in my overcoat pocket and as I was starting he insisted that I didn't balance properly and he crammed one into the pocket on the other side. To resist would be affectation and I submitted.[4]

There seems to be little question that Fort Bridger's first citizen, Judge Carter, was an unusual man in many ways. Little wonder that his fame spread and a county was named for him by the Dakota legislature in 1867. However, when Wyoming territory was organized in 1868, the first session of the territorial legislature changed the name from Carter to Sweetwater County with South Pass City as County seat. This seemed a rather ungrateful act considering Carter's long years of service and the fact that he was credited with influencing the transfer of the Fort Bridger area from Utah to the newly created Wyoming territory.

When Uinta county was organized in 1869, Governor John Campbell of Wyoming appointed J. Van Carter, a son-in-law of Judge Carter, as county clerk

Judge William Carter, "Mr. Fort Bridger," dominated the fort forty years.

148

and then appointed Judge Carter himself to be county treasurer and probate judge. In October 1870 Judge W. A. Carter was appointed post trader of the fort by the secretary of war, and so he continued to have considerable influence.

Judge Carter was disappointed when the decision was made by the Union Pacific Railroad to bypass Fort Bridger. His daughter, Lulie Carter Groshon, claimed that she understood the original plan was to include Fort Bridger on the railroad route, but the route was changed by "one of the principle locating engineers, who couldn't obtain a quart of whiskey there on Sunday." Whatever the reason, the railroad was constructed nine miles to the north, and Judge Carter had to be content with the establishment of Carter's Station as a stopping place. However, he was able to get a road and a telegraph line built to connect Fort Bridger with the Union Pacific at Carter's Station.

Judge William Alexander Carter continued to be the dominating force of Fort Bridger until his death in 1881. Commanding officers were only temporary residents but Judge Carter with his stately appearance, renowned hospitality, and widespread business interests was the most important person at the post during the 1860s and 1870s. In fact, many people called it "Carter's Fort" rather than Fort Bridger.

Archibald Geilsie, a British official who was a guest of the fort in 1879, discussed the history of Fort Bridger, and after mentioning the run-down condition of the buildings, summarized the position of Judge Carter in a rather interesting way:

Judge Carter, who used to be the patriarch of the district still lives at this post, combining in his own worthy person the office of postmaster, merchant, farmer, cattle owner, judge and general benefactor of all who claim his hospitality. His well known integrity has gained him the respect of white man and red man alike, and we found his name a kind of household word all through the west.[5]

The British visitor might have added a few other roles that the judge played during this period. He served as something of a public relations man for Fort Bridger. While taking his annual visits to his home in Virginia, he spent much time in the nation's capital and had many friends among public men of the day. While there, he spread the story of the delightful summer climate and the opportunities for sport and recreation that Fort Bridger offered. As a result, his home was filled in the summer with friends and their ladies who enjoyed the gracious hospitality of his charming wife and family. Visitors to the post made up camping parties and engaged guides for trips into the Uinta Mountains. The scenery was beautiful and the fishing and hunting were excellent.

A most important role for Judge Carter was that of husband and father. He was the father of four daughters and two sons. The discovery of several letters

Judge Carter's schoolhouse and other buildings built for the family still stand.

written to his wife while he was on trips to Washington reveal him to be a very thoughtful and loving husband. Their home was the center of culture and entertainment. Often, with good musicians among the troops, there were dances and musical entertainments. His Steinway piano, which had been hauled across the plains by ox teams before the building of the railroad, not only served for dances but was also used by local artists as well as distinguished musicians who were visiting. His excellent library was also an attraction. Part of this library and his old piano are now in the possession of the state university at Laramie. The little schoolhouse still standing on the grounds of the state museum at Fort Bridger was Judge Carter's private family schoolhouse. He provided high-class instructors and many educational opportunities for his four daughters and two sons so they might be able to enter college.

The result was that the home of Judge Carter at Fort Bridger was the scene of much recreation and cultural activity, making Fort Bridger a much sought after station by the military personnel. Through this long association with the army and the marriage of two of his daughters to army officers, Judge Carter's home was looked upon as the center for military men in the area.

But Judge Carter was first and primarily a merchant, and he conducted a very successful operation at Fort Bridger. He first built a home, a store, and some warehouses. In order to do this, he erected a mill in the Uintas some 50

150

miles to the south where he had his men prepare lumber for the buildings at Fort Bridger. He also located an excellent deposit of limestone a dozen miles to the west which was used for the primary foundations of his buildings. Carter had good connections with Robert Campbell of St. Louis and was able to buy supplies from him. Goods were shipped to Atchinson, Kansas, the end of the rail line, and from there to Fort Bridger by way of ox teams. In 1860, for example, he bought goods on credit in St. Louis amounting to over $100,000, including farm machinery and implements. The cost of wagon transportation alone was over $50,000, but in six months the Judge was able to pay off this amount by the sale of goods at Fort Bridger. He purchased all sorts of supplies including woolen shirts, blouses, woolen socks, men's woolens, fine toilet soaps, German cologne, combs—in fact almost every kind of item that would help to make life more endurable on the frontier. Of course, there was a large supply of staple groceries, such as sugar, flour, coffee, bacon, and dried fruit. Being postmaster, he also had to keep a steady supply of stamps.[6] One important item that was assuredly sought by weary travelers when they came to Fort Bridger was some alcoholic beverage to warm them up and ease their aching bones. Judge Carter was able to supply this need. For example, one order dated May 1860 read as follows:

The Langton whiskey purchased from you last season has been pronounced the finest whiskey in Utah. I would be obliged to you to send me 40 barrels of Bourbon Whiskey of the same quality and price. Please be particular as to the quality as I would not have the poisonous compound generally brought into this country.[7]

He expanded his business interests into farming, cattle raising, mill owning, and almost every other aspect of business enterprise that could be operated on the frontier.

Another role as important as those of sutler, merchant, and businessman was that of justice of the peace and probate judge. Although he had no training as a lawyer, Judge Carter was regarded highly by the military leaders who found him to be a man of great honesty, integrity, and sound judgment. When Judge Burr resigned from the position of justice of the peace in 1858, Carter was assigned to that position. Governor Cumming named him probate judge in 1858 and he was reappointed to that office year after year without a break until Fort Bridger became part of the newly organized Wyoming territory. This position was rather unique in Utah territory, because two early federal judges, unhappy with their experience with the Mormon hierarchy, left the region, and the territorial legislature had given criminal and civil powers to the probate courts. These courts retained this power until the Poland Act restored the power to the federal courts in 1874. Thus, during all of the time that Judge Carter served as probate judge, he had the power to exercise original jurisdiction over civil and criminal cases as well as in chancery at common law.

151

Fort Bridger was a fairly busy post at this time, and since there always seemed to be people on the frontier who felt that they could steal from others without being apprehended, Judge Carter was required to render judgment in numerous cases. Many had to do with the stealing of horses, mules, harnesses, various bits of food, and other supplies that were vital to people crossing the continent. One interesting case involving the stealing of animals was initiated by George K. Otis who was the Fort Bridger agent of the Ben Holladay stage line at the time. He filed a complaint charging Rodney Babbitt and Thomas Watson with the theft of two valuable mules from the stable at the fort. The jury convicted them the next day and Judge Carter sentenced the men to two years' imprisonment in the territorial prison—the minimum punishment under the law. In the language of the court, the officers were instructed to deliver the "bodies of Rodney Babbitt and Thomas Watson to the warden in Salt Lake City, where the penitentiary was located." Although they were chained hand and foot Babbitt succeeded in breaking his foot chains and tried to escape. The officers who were accompanying him speedily shot him. They wondered what they should do next, but finding in their writ that they were to deliver the bodies of the prisoners to the sheriff in Salt Lake City, they took their instructions literally and stowed the body in the stage coach and duly delivered it to the destination.

Carter presided over the cases involving divorce, murder, and almost every type of crime that was committed on the frontier. On one occasion, four soldiers accused of killing a Mr. Harris were sent to Camp Floyd, but were returned to Judge Carter to be taken care of. He wrote: "Having no place to keep them I was obliged to let them go at liberty. That night in company of two deserting local soldiers and stolen livestock they fled the valley." Carter was very upset with this breakdown of justice and he wrote to the governor: "I am at a loss to know how to proceed the case. If a great community of men has not a right to make laws for its own preservation, brute force and crime must remain supreme. I shall endeavor to at least keep up a show of authority until some salutary measures have been adopted."[8] The statement shows the sense of responsibility of Judge Carter whose instinct for decency had been very much aroused. Carter was of course different from many western justices who often were ignorant of the law and not much above the criminal element that they were trying. In Professor Davis's study of western justice, Judge Carter received a high rating:[9]

As the local judge near the center of it all, the annals of the region might well remember that William A. Carter, like many others of his kind, kept faith and high principle to place the priceless stamp of integrity on law and justice of his locale. It scarce needs saying that physical security for the individual, one's family and the community in the pioneer west did not spring up all in a moment or come about simply as a matter of course. It had to be built

Carter and his family were buried in this private cemetery at the fort.

conscientiously and deliberately through years of unfailing devotion to public interests by a man like Judge Carter at Fort Bridger.

Judge Carter, in addition to his interest in business and his activities as a judge, was pony express agent, postmaster, and custodian of government funds which he dispersed regularly to officers and soldiers and others. He was his own bookkeeper and was a very careful and exact one. He also rendered a great service to the post by attempting to understand and win the friendship of the Indians. The Shoshone Indians from the north and the Utes from their reservation to the southeast passed through Fort Bridger at least twice a year on exchange visits and always stopped for a day's trading. The Indians called Judge Carter "Totesee-motesee" meaning "grey beard" because of his flowing white beard. He and chief Washakie of the Shoshones were best friends, each holding the other in high regard. Major Andrew S. Burt, who was the commanding officer at Fort Bridger in 1866, told Judge Carter's son William the following story:

At a time when government troops were engaged in Northeastern Wyoming in a battle with the Indians from several tribes, Washakee kept his warriors from joining in the fight. In recognition of his services, the war department sent out a fine saddle to be given to the chief for his friendly cooperation. A day was set for the presentation, a mixed crowd was assembled in front of Judge Carter's

153

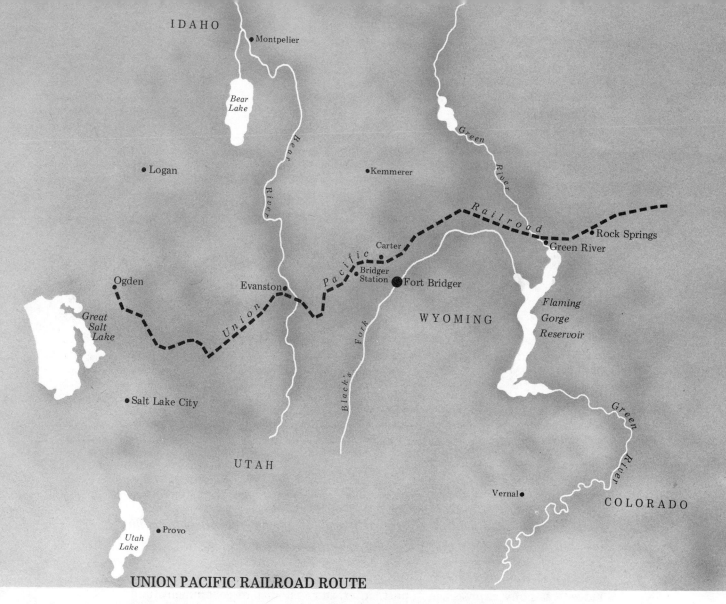

UNION PACIFIC RAILROAD ROUTE

store and the officer delivered his prepared speech. He then placed his hand on the saddle and claimed it a gift from the great white father in Washington. But Washakee would have none of it. He made no move to accept the gift nor did he make any reply to the big talk. It was finally discovered that he would only receive the saddle if it were tendered to him by his friend "Totesee-motesee," the Indian name for Judge Carter.[10]

Ironically, Judge Carter's death resulted, indirectly at least, in an effort to aid his Indian friends. In the spring of 1880 the U.S. Government was considering the removal of the White River Utes from Colorado to the Uinta reservation in Northeastern Utah. The War Department ordered that Fort Bridger be regarrisoned because of its proximity to the Ute reservation and because of the needed quarters for troops while the other fort which was planned on the south side of the Uinta Mountains was being constructed. Judge Carter was given credit for this reoccupation of Fort Bridger. In army circles at the time it was often called "Carter's Fort" because of Carter's long and influential career at the post. When this order for the reestablishment of

154

Fort Bridger was given, Judge Carter was instrumental in bringing to the attention of the commanding officer the practicability of making a wagon road across the Uinta Mountains to the proposed site of the new post, which would be a much shorter and more direct route than the one then used by way of Park City, Utah. There were two trails in use by the Uinta Ute Indians between the reservation and Fort Bridger. One crossed immediately west of Gilbert Peak and was known as the Soldiers' Trail because it was said to have been used by General Marcy in 1857 on his trip to New Mexico to get supplies for Albert S. Johnston's troops. The other, known as the Lodge Pole Route, ran from a point near present-day Burntfork in Wyoming to Ashley, Utah. In the summer of 1881, Commander General George Crook, Department of the Platte, made an inspection trip across the mountains from Fort Bridger to the Uinta Ute Agency. He found the Gilbert Peak trail impractical for a wagon road and so decided upon the Lodge Pole Trail as advised by Judge Carter. Since there was some delay in building the road. Judge Carter undertook at his own expense the work of making a passable road along the designated route, expecting that it would be adopted and improved later by the War Department. As the winter of 1881-82 was approaching, there was no time for surveys. He and his crew had to bridge streams, corduroy marshes, clear a roadway through timbered sections, and construct two long and difficult dugways. As a result of hardships suffered in this enterprise, Judge Carter was taken sick at his camp on the stream named Carter Creek after him, and died shortly afterwards of pleurisy in his home at Fort Bridger on 7 November 1881. Thus ended the life of a remarkable man who left his stamp not only on Fort Bridger but also upon the territory and state of Wyoming.

According to Edgar Carter, son of the famous judge, William A. Carter was not fond of Jim Bridger. He said that Bridger's excessive egoism was wearying. His many stories of encounters with Indians and bears were hardly believable, and he claimed credit for all the explorations west of the Missouri River. The Judge said that Bridger was densely ignorant, being unable to read or write, and that he had lived so long with the Indians that he had absorbed all their cunning and duplicity.

Another longtime resident of Fort Bridger, but with a better reputation than Jim Bridger, was Jack Robinson, usually known as Uncle Jack, although his real name was John Robertson. He had been living on the frontier for almost forty years and had adopted many of the habits of the Indians, including marriage to several Indian wives. During the summer he lived in an Indian lodge, and in winter in a log cabin a few miles from the fort. An unknown army officer described Uncle Jack:

. . . as a gentleman . . . one of those characters who has the instincts and character of a gentleman place him where you may. His associations made him great in that you will always find cropping out those qualities that indicate him as

155

Often mistaken for Jim Bridger, Jack Robinson's real name was Robertson.

Uncle Jack Robinson's gravestone located in the Carter private cemetery.

intended for a different sphere of life and mark that he would have made under different circumstances. By 1866 he was 65 years old, and hale and hearty though of course not as active as in his early life. But he was a constant visitor at Fort Bridger and well known for his storytelling of legends of the region. He was mistaken for Jim Bridger.[11]

Uncle Jack was buried in the Fort Bridger Cemetery.

People determine the character of a community, and Fort Bridger had some interesting characters residing there over the years—Bridger, Vasquez, Robison, Johnston, Forney, Luther Mann, Washakie, Robertson, and Carter, but the most influential of these was Carter.

12

Many old military buildings such as these are still standing at the fort.

Fort Bridger becomes a state historical park

The decision of the army to phase out Fort Bridger in 1890 left the post in a state of limbo for a number of years. There was still some dispute concerning the ownership of the fort, since Jim Bridger's heirs were still pressing their claims for redress because of the failure of the government to pay Bridger the amount of rent agreed upon in the contract of 1858. The Mormon claims were dependent upon the validity of Bridger's ownership since they had purchased the post from the mountaineer in 1855.

Validity of Ownership Claims
It was not until 1869, twelve years after Bridger had leased Fort Bridger to the U.S., that he began inquiring of the War Department as to whether or not the government intended to pay him $6,000, the sum of ten annual rental payments which he claimed due to him under terms of the lease. Receiving no reply, he sent another letter on 6 January 1870 to remind the secretary of war that the lease of 1857 also gave the U.S. government the option of purchasing Fort Bridger for $10,000. He mentioned that if the government did not wish to take advantage of this option he would like to be restored to peaceful possession of the fort. On April 25 of the same year, the War Department replied that as soon as Bridger produced evidence of his title to the fort the government would carry into effect the agreement made with him in 1857. Apparently Bridger made no effort to establish title, but the War Department made inquiries of the general land office, and in 1872 the commissioner of that office

159

The ice house and storage shed built by Judge Carter at Fort Bridger.

declared that no private survey or claim such as Bridger's was recognized in the vicinity of Fort Bridger.

In 1873 Bridger was urged by friends and family to solicit the aid of General Benjamin F. Butler, senator from Massachusetts, who had a reputation for being concerned with the oppressed. Failing to get satisfaction from the War Department, Bridger wrote to the senator hoping to use his political influence, but there is no evidence that Butler acted upon the plea or even that he received the letter or replied to it.

Bridger's family then decided to take the situation in hand and in January 1878 made formal inquiry of the secretary of war in regards to the status of Bridger's claims. They also asked to be paid the cumulative amount owed to them. In February 1878 the secretary of war informed Bridger's family that his failure to establish the title to the property in question previous to it being embraced in a military reservation excluded the secretary of war from recognizing his claim to ownership and rent.

Receiving no satisfaction from the War Department, Bridger's family hired attorney Charles M. Carter to pursue their claims in Congress. They finally obtained a hearing in May 1880 at which time the House Committee on Claims, co-operating with the corresponding senate committee, asked the War Department to investigate and report on Bridger's claims. Bridger died in July 1881

The military building at left houses the present Bureau of Information.

before the investigation was completed, but his family continued to pursue the case from 1880 to 1889 at which time a complete report of the investigation was presented by quartermaster general S. A. Holaberg. Knowing that the War Department did not recognize Bridger's claims to the title of the fort by grant from the governor of upper California, Carter decided it was hopeless to press the claim and decided to base the source of title to the fort on an alleged grant from the Governor of Chihuahua whose records would probably be difficult to obtain. Carter also alleged that Bridger was a citizen of Mexico and was entitled to have his rights recognized by the Treaty of Peace under rules of international law that state that conquered nations cannot dispose of the private rights of the conquered subjects. However, since Carter could not produce evidence of title from the Mexican government, the committee did not feel that they could apply the rule of international law. Carter also presented the fact that Bridger had been in the mountains all of his life and was ignorant of the steps required to perfect his title, thus appealing to their sympathy. However, after hearing all the testimony, the congressional committee accepted the quartermaster's investigations and recommended that the condition of the contract had not been fulfilled, thus precluding any claimant from recovery.

After denying Bridger's claim to ownership, the Congress considered the question of payment for improvements which were supposed to have been erected by the claimant. The improvements were said to consist of the construction of thirteen log houses still located at the fort, all of which were surrounded by a stone wall about eighteen feet high and five feet thick laid in cement. Carter also described a corral for stock that was enclosed by a wall laid in cement, and he wrote about six other outhouses. A casual investigation revealed that such a claim was not valid. The only thing that was left standing when the army arrived was the cement wall. Carter's affidavits, gathered from men who testified in Bridger's behalf, were made many years later, and these men either had been dishonest or were confused about the conditions at Fort Bridger when the army arrived. The congressional committee was not fooled by Carter's tactics and awarded $6,000 for the only improvement standing at the time of the arrival of the army—the cement wall. Interestingly enough, the cement wall accredited to Bridger had been built by the Mormons. Finally, in 1899, the heirs of Jim Bridger received $6,000 for a wall which he did not build.

Lewis Robison's claims, though much more complicated, can be disposed of more easily since his claim to any compensation from the government would depend on recognition of Bridger's claim by the government. Robison, as agent for the Mormon Church, had obtained ownership of Fort Bridger by purchasing it from James Bridger and Lewis Vasquez. He had tried to reassert his claims of ownership in July 1861, when the post was being all but abandoned because of the Civil War, and surplus property was being sold, but Robison's claims to ownership were not acceptable and the sale was held as scheduled.

For the next sixteen years Robison did nothing more about his claims to Fort Bridger. He still had in his possession deed to the fort given to him by Brigham Young in 1858. Of course, during this time Fort Bridger had become an active military post and Robison's claims were apparently forgotten by the government officials. However, in 1877, shortly before Brigham Young's death, the issue was reactivated when Mormon leaders, in trying to get Young's affairs settled, called upon Robison to return the deed to Fort Bridger to him. There was no question that Robison was obligated to return the deed to the Church, since Fort Bridger had been purchased with Church money. But although Robison had acted for the Church in purchasing the fort, he had also entered into a partnership with Brigham Young on a half-and-half basis for any profits that might be acquired during his supervision of the fort. After considerable negotiations, on the basis that he should have received some of these profits, Lewis Robison signed the following document in February 1878:

Received from John Taylor, trustee-in-trust, for the Church of Jesus Christ of Latter-day Saints, the sum of $1260, the sum being in full payment of all accounts, claims, and demands I have against the said trustee-in-trust or agent connected with said Church of Jesus Christ of Latter-day Saints up to this date.

Followed by some legal statements, the document concludes:

162

From behind the Bureau one can see the old wall built by Lewis Robison.

the deed from me to Brigham Young for Bridger's ranch, with all the papers mentioned in said deed attached, the following being a copy. This indenture made the 18th of July.

It is interesting to note that John Taylor, President of the Mormon Church, returned to Robison this indenture that he had signed and given to Brigham Young in 1877. This deed was only recognized by the Church and had no legality in the courts or on the records of the territory. This is why in a letter concerning the deed dated 22 January 1878, Robison said, "With this understanding that the deed be returned to me, as I understand it, it has not been recorded nor inventoried so as to appear anywhere in record." John Taylor, the President of the Church, signed a paper that

Relinquished any right or title or interests that he may have to the land and premises known as Fort Bridger, situated in Uinta County in the territory of Wyoming and said to have contained 400 square miles of ground, more or less, also hereby relinquishing claims of law or equity against said Bridger ranch property by reasons of advances made or otherwise including ranch issues or profits accumulated up to or from the date thereof. [Signed by] John Taylor, trustee-in-trust for the Church of Jesus Christ of Latter-day Saints.[2]

163

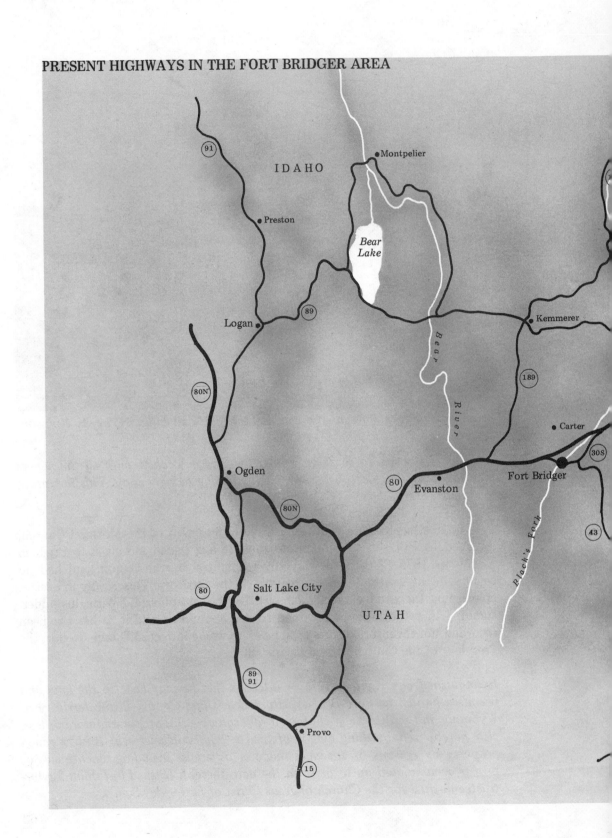

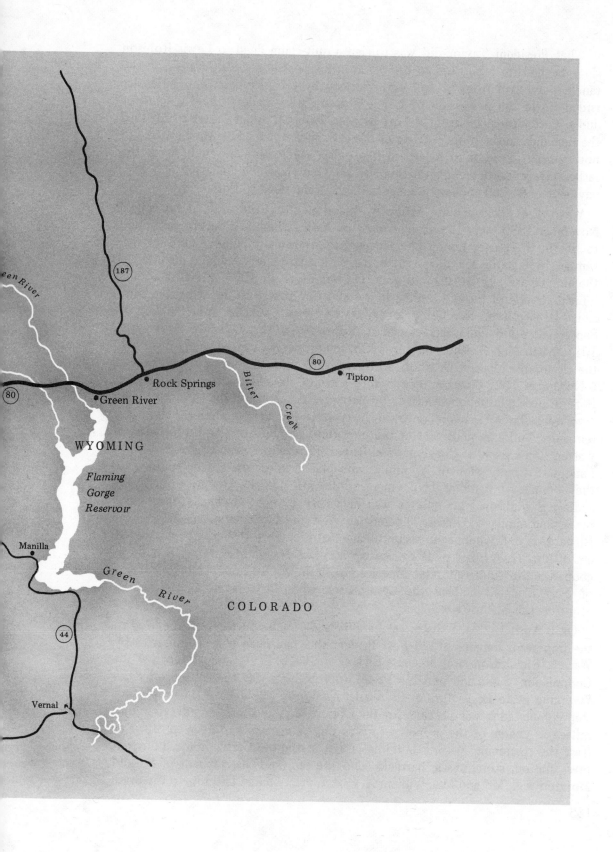

What President Taylor did was to sign a quit-claim deed to Lewis Robison since he had no legal deed to the ranch in his possession. So the deed to the ranch, purchased from Bridger and Vasquez by the Mormon Church, finally ended up in the possession of Lewis Robison who made formal demand of Judge Carter for possession of Fort Bridger. Robison asked Carter to forward the demands to the proper officer of the U.S. government, but when Carter did not comply, Robison was left to take what satisfaction he could from the rather meager settlement given him by the Church which consisted of a cash payment of $1,260 and an unrecognized quit-claim deed to Fort Bridger.

When Fort Bridger was officially abandoned by the U.S. Army on 6 November 1890 Mary E. Carter, widow of Judge William A. Carter, continued to live in the Carter home. She received a government patent dated 11 November 1896 giving her title to the home, sutlers store, and the land included in the immediate site of the old fort. On her death in 1904, the title to the immediate site of the old trading house and fort passed to her daughter, Mrs. Lucy L. Groshon. The latter conveyed the property to M. Ada Carson, 24 September 1906, who reconveyed it, however, to Mrs. Groshon in January 1911. When Mrs. Groshon died in 1925, the property reverted to her husband, the Honorable Maurice Groshon, who was residing in the old Carter home. On 5 November 1926 Groshon sold twenty acres of the old site to W. C. Casto of Fort Bridger who reconveyed the property to Mr. Groshon on 14 June 1928. Two weeks later, Groshon conveyed thirty and a half acres embracing all of the remaining buildings and most of the important portions of the old fort site to Warren Richardson of Cheyenne and Robert Ellison of Casper of the Historical Landmark Commission of Wyoming, who placed in escrow a deed running to the Commission pending the payment by them of the purchase price of $7,100 and such additional amount as was necessary to cover interests, insurance, taxes, and similar expenses. The keen interest and initiative of commissioners Richardson and Weppner in securing this historic site together with the valued aid of Mrs. H. J. Boice of Rock Springs and Roy Mason of Kemmerer, and the cooperation of the Honorable Maurice Groshon, W. A. Carter, and W. C. Casto of Fort Bridger, enabled the Commission to make substantial progress in acquiring this historic site.

On 3 April 1929 the Historical Landmark Commission received the deed to the important remains of old Fort Bridger that had been placed in escrow by Warren Richardson and Robert Ellison in 1928. This acquisition by the Commission was made possible by an appropriation for that purpose by the Wyoming State Legislature at its regular session in 1929. With this important step completed it was possible for the Commission and its local advisory committee in charge of the property to find ways and means to keep in repair at least the remaining historic buildings, such as the old Carter home, pony express station, storehouses, barracks, and the jail, and the remnant of the old Mormon wall. Mr. and Mrs. William A. Carter, Jr., donated two lots to the State of Wyoming adjacent to the entrance to the fort grounds in order to protect the entrance for all time against mercenary establishments in June 1929. The following year, a little over six additional acres were purchased from W. C. Casto. This tract included the old officers row and the street in front, and the location of the bandstand site.

It was decided to house the museum in the old men's quarters, a T-shaped building built in the 1880s. By refinishing the interior and strengthening the walls with cement footing, the committee felt that it could house the hundreds of relics that had been collected. A concrete floor was laid throughout the building and a red tile roof was installed. Heating the huge structure and building display cases were added expenses.

In July 1954 a valuable addition was made to the museum when Judge Carter's son, Edgar N. Carter, who was born at Fort Bridger eighty-one years before, announced that he was presenting a model of Fort Bridger to the museum. Construction of this scale model took eighteen months and was valued at $1,000. Edgar Carter, who was a charter member of the Westerners, an organization of western history buffs, supplemented his own intimate knowledge of the fort—his boyhood home—with intensive research into archives and government documents. The result has been the faithful reproduction of the old officers' quarters, the barracks, the guardhouses, hospital, bandstand, pony express stable and sheds, milk house, and all the buildings used by Johnston's Army. The Ellingsford Contractors of Evanston built an eight- by twelve-foot table to display the model—which as well as buildings, included trees, sidewalks, and streams.

At present Fort Bridger is designated as a Historical Park and State Museum and is operated jointly by the Museum Division, Wyoming State Archives and Historical Department, which is in charge of the exhibits and displays, and the Wyoming Recreation Commission which takes care of the grounds, building exteriors, and personnel. It is open to the public free of charge seven days a week from April to October. There were in excess of 57,000 visitors in 1973.

The State of Wyoming is to be commended for its efforts to preserve this historic site and to help American as well as foreign visitors to understand and appreciate the great heritage received from the men and women who pioneered the exploration and colonization of the trans-Mississippi West. Fort Bridger is a symbol of that heritage.

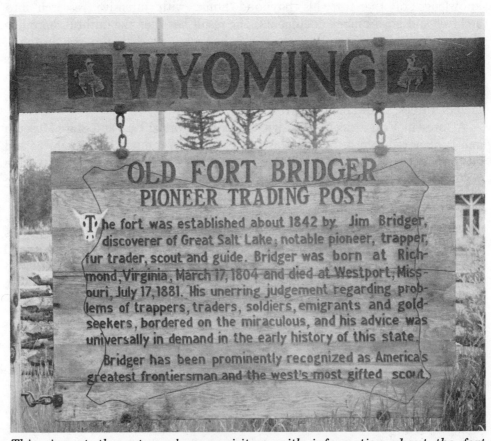

This sign at the gate welcomes visitors with information about the fort.

Notes

Chapter 1

1. Hiram Martin Chittenden, *The American Fur Trade of the Far West*, 2 vols. (New York: Press of the Pioneers, Inc., 1935), vol. 1, p. 261.

2. Charles L. Camp, *James Clyman, Frontiersman* (Portland, Oregon: Champoeg Press, 1960), p. 15.

3. Ibid., pp. 57-60.

4. Samuel Parker, *Journal of an Exploring Tour beyond the Rocky Mountains* (Ithaca, New York: Andrus, Woodruff and Countlett, 1844), pp. 80-81.

5. Alfred Jacob Miller, *The West of Alfred Jacob Miller* (Norman: University of Oklahoma Press, 1967), p. 159.

6. Bernard A. Devoto, *Across the Wide Missouri* (Boston: Houghton Mifflin, 1967), p. 378.

7. A. G. Brackett, "Fort Bridger," (unpublished manuscript, 1870, special collections, Harold B. Lee Library, BYU, Provo, Utah), p. 4.

8. Grenville Mellen Dodge, *Biographical Sketch of James Bridger* (New York: Unz and Co., 1905), pp. 5-6.

9. Edwin Bryant, *What I Saw in California* (Palo Alto: Lewis Osborne, 1967), pp. 142-44.

10. Joel Palmer, *Journal of Travels over the Rocky Mountains to the Mouth of the Columbia River* (Cincinnati: J. A. and U. P. James, 1847), p. 35.

11. John McBride, ed., *Overland in 1846* (Georgetown, California: Talisman Press, 1963), p. 96.

Chapter 2

1. Overton Johnson and William H. Winter, *Route across the Rocky Mountains* (Princeton: Princeton University Press, 1932), p. 15.

2. John Boardman, "Journal of John Boardman," *Utah State Historical Quarterly*, 2(October, 1929): 102.

3. Charles Carey, ed., *Journal of Theodore Talbot*, 1843, 1849-1852 (Portland: Metropolitan Press, 1931), pp. 41-42.

4. Captain J. C. Fremont, *Report of the Exploring Expedition to the Rocky Mountains in the Year 1842* (Washington, D.C.: Gales and Seaton Printers, 1845), p. 130.

5. Joseph E. Ware, *The Emigrants' Guide to California* (Princeton: Princeton University Press, 1932), pp. 25-26.

6. Edwin Bryant, *Rocky Mountain Adventures* (New York: Hurst and Co., 1885), pp. 142-44.

7. Biographical Sketch of An Early Pioneer (unpublished manuscript, Bancroft Library, Berkeley, California).

8. Bryant, *Rocky Mountain Adventures*, pp. 142-44.

9. Eliza P. Donner Houghton, *The Expedition of the Donner Party and Its Tragic Fate* (Chicago: A. C. McClurg and Son, 1911), pp. 31-32.

10. McBride, *Overland*, pp. 279-80.

Chapter 3

1. Journal History of The Church of Jesus Christ of Latter-day Saints (LDS Church Historical Department), p. 1; hereafter referred to as Journal History. It was during this conversation that Bridger criticized the Fremont maps the Mormons were using to aid them, and is reputed to have made his famous offer to pay $1,000 for the first ear of corn raised in Salt Lake Valley. On 8 July 1849 in the Journal History the following is found: "the mountaineers never thought we could raise corn here, Mr. Bridger says he would give a thousand dollars per bushell of all the corn we could raise in the valley." It is interesting that part of this statement has been rubbed out and someone has written in pencil, "This is edited wrong." The right version is on the opposite page which reads, "Mr. Bridger says he would give $1000.00 if he only knew if we could raise an ear of corn." This is signed by Andrew Jenson and William Lund as being correct.

2. Kate B. Carter, ed., *Heart Throbs of the West* (Salt Lake City: Daughters of the Utah Pioneers), 6:296-300.

3. Matthias F. Cowley, *Wilford Woodruff* (Salt Lake City: Bookcraft, 1964), pp. 308-9.

4. *Millennial Star*, 1 June 1840, pp. 162-63.

5. Preston Nibley, *Exodus to Greatness* (Salt Lake City: Deseret News Press, 1947), p. 414.

6. Juanita Brooks and Robert Glass Cleland, *A Mormon Chronicle* (San Marino, California: Huntington Library, 1955) 1:77-78.

7. Journal History, 5 October 1848, p. 1.

8. Peter Decker, *The Diaries of Peter Decker* (Georgetown, California: Talisman Press, 1966), pp. 97-98.

9. Dale L. Morgan, "Washakie and the Shoshoni," *Annals of Wyoming* 25(Cheyenne: Wyoming State Historical Society, 1955): 152.

Chapter 4

1. *Annual Report to the Commissioner of Indian Affairs*, 1849-1850 (Washington, D.C.: Gideone & Co., 1850), p. 66.

2. Morgan, "Washakie," 25:158.

3. *Annual Report*, 1849-50, p. 68.

4. Howard Stansbury, *An Expedition to the Valley of the Great Salt Lake* (Philadelphia: Lippincott, Grambo and Co., 1852), p. 76.

5. 21 July 1848, Fort Bridger Collection, LDS Church Historical Department, Salt Lake City.

6. Journal History, 7 May 1849, p. 1
7. Ibid.
8. Journal History, 15 June 1849, p. 1.
9. Morgan, "Washakie," 25:183.
10. Ibid., 26:66.
11. History of Brigham Young (unpublished manuscript, LDS Church Historical Department, Salt Lake City), p. 1.
12. *Utah Territorial Legislature, Acts, Resolutions and Memorials, Passed by the Legislature, Assembly of the Territory of Utah* (Salt Lake City, 1852), pp. 166-67.
13. Morgan, "Washakie," 26:142.
14. Journal History, 14 October 1852, p. 1.
15. Morgan, "Washakie," 26:144-45.
16. Ibid., 26:144.

Chapter 5

1. William A. Hickman, *Brigham Young's Destroying Angel* (New York: George A. Crofutt, 1872), p. 91.
2. Jim Bridger (unpublished manuscript in Utah state archives, Salt Lake City) and information on subpoena.
3. Leland H. Creer, *Utah and the Nation* (Seattle: University of Washington Press, 1929), p. 81.
4. J. Cecil Alter, *James Bridger* (Salt Lake City: Shepard Book Co., 1925), pp. 247-48.
5. Thomas Flint, *Diary of Dr. Thomas Flint* (Los Angeles: Historical Society of Southern California, 1925), p. 45.
6. Journal History, 17 October 1853, p. 1.
7. Randolf B. March, *Thirty Years of Army Life on the Border* (Philadelphia: Lippincott, 1963), p. 363.
8. U. S. Congress, *Senate Report*, No. 625, 52nd Cong., 1st sess., 1892, p. 12.
9. Receipt, 18 October 1858, Fort Bridger Collection.
10. History of Brigham Young, p. 2.
11. James S. Brown, *Life of a Pioneer* (Salt Lake City: George Q. Cannon & Sons Co., 1900), p. 306.
12. Ibid., pp. 307-8.
13. Hosea Stout, Diary (unpublished manuscript, special collections, Harold B. Lee Library, BYU, Provo, Utah) 7, 11 May 1854.

Chapter 6

1. *Utah Territorial Legislature, Acts* (1852), pp. 161-64.
2. Morgan, "Washakie," 26:160.
3. Ibid., 26:158-59.
4. Andrew Jenson, "History of Fort Bridger and Fort Supply," *Utah Genealogical and Historical Magazine*, 4 (1913):49.
5. Blank Contract, Fort Bridger Collection.
6. Indenture, 3 August 1855, Fort Bridger Collection.
7. Salt Lake County records, book B, Salt Lake City, p. 127.
8. Receipt, 3 August 1855, Fort Bridger Collection. (*See* page 175 for inventory ledger.)
9. Receipt, 20 October 1858, Fort Bridger Collection.
10. Hickman, *Destroying Angel*, p. 118.
11. Brigham Young, Letter book, 2 (unpublished manuscript, LDS Church Historical

Department, Salt Lake City):296.

12. Journal History, 21 August 1855, p. 1.

13. Brigham Young, Letter book, 2:889.

14. Lewis Robison to Daniel H. Wells, 19 August 1856, Lewis Robison Collection, LDS Church Historical Department, Salt Lake City, p. 603.

15. Brigham Young to Lewis Robison, 2 June 1857, History of Brigham Young.

16. Ibid., p. 757.

17. Ibid., p. 1015.

18. Ibid., p. 1017.

19. W. G. Johnston, *Experience of a Forty Niner* (Pittsburgh, 1892), pp. 163-66.

20. Stansbury, *Expedition to the Great Salt Lake*, p. 74.

21. Irene D. Paden, ed., *A Journal of Madison Berryman Moorman, 1850-1851* (San Francisco: California Historical Society, 1948), p. 45.

22. John Wood, Journal (microcard, Harold B. Lee Library, BYU, Provo, Utah) pp. 36-37.

23. Harriet Sherrill, *Prairie Schooner Lady: The Journal of Harriet Sherrill* (Los Angeles: Westernlore Press, 1959), p. 107.

24. Thomas Flint, *Diary of Dr. Thomas Flint* (Los Angeles: Historical Society of Southern California, 1925), p. 45.

25. Frederick Hawkins Piercy, *Route From Liverpool to Great Salt Lake Valley*, ed. Fawn Brodie (Harvard: Harvard University Press, 1962), p. 124.

26. C. G. Coutant, *History of Wyoming and the Far West* (Laramie: Chaplin Spafford and Mathison, Printers, 1899), p. 353.

27. Milton R. Hunter, *Brigham Young the Colonizer* (Salt Lake City: Deseret News Press, 1940), p. 288.

28. Lewis Robison to Daniel H. Wells, 21 July 1856, Lewis Robison Collection.

29. Lewis Robison to Daniel H. Wells, 30 May 1857, Lewis Robison Collection.

30. Lewis Robison to Brigham Young, 11 July 1847, Lewis Robison Collection.

31. Journal History, 3 October 1857, p. 2.

32. John Pulsipher, Diary (unpublished manuscript, special collections, Harold B. Lee Library, BYU, Provo, Utah).

Chapter 7

1. License, 20 October 1855, Lewis Robison Collection.

2. Brigham Young to Isaac Bullock, Brigham Young, Letter book, 2:835.

3. Morgan, "Washakie," 26:182-85.

4. William A. Hickman, Isaac Bullock, and Lewis Robison to Brigham Young, 19 August 1856, Isaac Bullock Collection, LDS Church Historical Department, Salt Lake City.

5. Lewis Robison to Daniel H. Wells, 23 August 1856, Lewis Robison Collection.

6. *Annual Report to the Commissioner of Indian Affairs*, 1856, pp. 224-26.

7. Lewis Robison to Daniel H. Wells, 19 August 1856, Lewis Robison Collection.

8. Lewis Robison to Brigham Young, 12 July 1857, Lewis Robison Collection.

9. Lewis Robison to Daniel H. Wells, 17 July 1856, Lewis Robison Collection.

10. Ibid.

11. Daniel H. Wells to Lewis Robison, 31 July 1856, Lewis Robison Collection.

12. Lewis Robison to Daniel H. Wells, 6 May 1856, Lewis Robison Collection.

13. Lewis Robison to Daniel H. Wells, 5 July 1856, Lewis Robison Collection.

14. Lewis Robison to Daniel H. Wells, 19 August 1856, Lewis Robison Collection.

15. Lewis Robison to Daniel H. Wells, 30 August 1856, Lewis Robison Collection.

16. Lewis Robison to Daniel H. Wells, 6 May 1856, Lewis Robison Collection.

17. Lewis Robison to Daniel H. Wells, 5 July 1856, Lewis Robison Collection.

18. Lewis Robison to Daniel H. Wells, 12 July 1857, Lewis Robison Collection.

19. Lewis Robison to Daniel H. Wells, 6 May 1856, Lewis Robison Collection.

20. Lewis Robison to Daniel H. Wells, 12 July 1856, Lewis Robison Collection.

21. Lewis Robison to Daniel H. Wells, 5 July 1856, Lewis Robison Collection.

22. LeRoy R. Hafen, *The Utah Expedition, 1857-58* (Glendale, California: Arthur H. Clark Co., 1958), p. 18.

23. Brigham Young to Lewis Robison, 4 August 1857, History of Brigham Young.

24. Brigham Young to Lewis Robison, 16 September 1857, Lewis Robison Collection.

25. Jenson, "History of Fort Bridger," 4:39.

26. Jesse W. Crosby, History and journal, 1820-1869 (unpublished manuscript, special collections, Harold B. Lee Library, BYU, Provo, Utah).

Chapter 8

1. Much of the material in the first three pages of this chapter is from Norman F. Furniss, *The Mormon Conflict* (New Haven, Connecticut: Yale University Press, 1960), chapter 5. Direct quotes are indicated and other information has been paraphrased.

2. Ralph P. Bieber, *Frontier Life in the Army* (Glendale, California: Arthur H. Clark Co., 1932), p. 217.

3. Furniss, *Mormon Conflict*, p. 163.

4. Ibid., p. 164.

5. Ibid., p. 195.

Chapter 9

1. Brackett, "Fort Bridger," p. 7. (*See* page 180 for list of commanding officers.)

2. Richard F. Burton, *The City of the Saints* (New York: Harper and Brothers, 1862), pp. 178-79.

3. Ibid.

4. Ibid.

5. *New York Herald*, 26 March 1860.

6. Lewis Robison to Daniel H. Wells, 17 July 1861, Lewis Robison Collection.

7. Notice issued by Lewis Robison, 22 July 1861, Fort Bridger Collection.

8. Robert S. Ellison, *Fort Bridger Wyoming, A Brief History* (Casper: Historical Landmark Commission of Wyoming, 1931), p. 37.

9. William E. Waters, *Life among the Mormons: And a March to Their Zion* (New York: Moorhead, Simpson and Bond, 1863), pp. 56-57.

10. General James T. Rusling, *Across America: or, The Great West and the Pacific Coast* (New York: Sheldon and Company, 1874), pp. 156-57.

11. Ellison, *Brief History*, p. 52.

12. Ibid., p. 53.

Chapter 10

1. Morgan, "Washakie," 27:61-88.

2. Ibid.

3. Ibid. (*See* page 174 for list of Indian agents.)

4. Coutant, *History of Wyoming*, p. 398.

5. Morgan, "Washakie," 28:200.

6. Ibid., p. 205.

7. Coutant, *History of Wyoming*, p. 412.

8. *The Annual Report of the Commissioner of Indian Affairs, 1865* (Washington, D.C.: Gideone & Co.), pp. 158-60.

9. Ibid., p. 160.

10. P. L. Williams, "Personal Recollections of Wash-a-kie Chief of the Shoshones," *Utah State Historical Quarterly* 1:4 (October 1928):101-2.

11. Ibid., p. 103.

12. *Annual Report*, 1870, pp. 644-45.

13. *Annual Report*, 1869, pp. 272-73.

14. *Annual Report*, 1871, p. 550.

15. *Annual Report*, 1878, p. 148.

Chapter 11

1. Burton, *City of the Saints*, p. 178.

2. Waters, *Life among the Mormons*, pp. 57-58.

3. Rusling, *Across America*, pp. 157-58.

4. Alexander Kelly McClure, *Three Thousand Miles through the Rocky Mountains* (Philadelphia: J. B. Lippincott, 1869), p. 149.

5. Ellison, *Brief History*, pp. 55-56.

6. William N. Carter, "Fort Bridger Days," *Westerners Brand Book* (Los Angeles, 1947):84-85.

7. Ibid., p. 85.

8. W. N. Davis, Jr., "Western Justice: The Court at Fort Bridger, Utah Territory," *Utah State Historical Quarterly* 23 (1955):118.

9. Ibid., p. 125.

10. Carter, "Fort Bridger Days," p. 85.

11. Waters, *Life among the Mormons,* p. 59.

Chapter 12

1. Statement of receipt, 15 February 1878, Lewis Robison Collection.

2. Statement of John Taylor, 15 February 1878, Fort Bridger Collection.

Appendix

Transcription from document on page 57

Property Belonging to Bridger and Vasques
Taken forcible possession of By the authorities of
Utah Territory, From 25th of August, to 1st November
1853.

Lewis Robison's receipt for Quartermaster and Commissary Stores; as Commissary and Quarter Master of Utah Territory.	$ 266.16
J. W. Cummins, Receipt as Capt Comm anding Fort Bridger Expedition	536.75
James Fergusons Receipts as Commander of Fort Bridger & Green river Expedition, For Guns. (and what he stiles contraband Indian Trade)	
Powder Ball Caps, of Knives	
39½ Doz Best quality Knives asserted 9.00 a Dz	355.50
17600 Caps 3.00 a thousand	52.80
25 N. W. Guns at 15.00 each	375.00
200 lbs. lead Balls 50^{cts} per lb	100.00
100 lbs powder 1.50 per lb	150.00
12 Rifle Guns; Some of them out of Repair $25.00	300.00
1 Black Smiths Anville	50.00
Iron and Steal used in Blacksmithing	50.00
Occupation of Fort and Houses near 2 months	500.00
	$2736.21

The above goods are charged at the established
prices of the Contry given under my hand this the
25th day of February 1854   James Bridger

Transcription from document on page 67

Fort Bridge   August 5th 1855

Dear Brothe

I arrived at F.T. Supply tusdyay Evening
an waited far Wm A Hickman to see what
was the best that could be done
He came to F. T. Supply on Wedensday Evening
an reporte Bridger verry carless and indeferent
about Selling. Stated that the Mountain
ears was trying to persuade him not to
Sell that all was Peace with him & the
Mormons an he had better keep the Peace

I came hear on thursday but soon
found that he would not fall on his
Price. I then told him that I was
ready to take him up at his office
Eight thousan Dollars & pay him as
he State he would take four thousan
Dollars down & wait fifteen months
for the ballence

He then wanted to invoice
Every thing on the place said it would
come to 6 or 8 hundred Dollars more
I just told him I would take him at
the offer he had made an not an other
Dime would I give. an that was Double
what he ever would git again.
He conclude he would take it

The next thing was the Security
Said he would take Bullock Wakely &
Jack Robison. I offere him as many
men at F. T. Supply as he might ask
But did not wish to ask Robison to
give my security
He said he would rather take a
Bond on the place than to take any men
for Security. He Also refuses to try
to obtain any title to the ranch more than
he knew has which is only Possession
He would not sign or except the papers
that I had. He Said he had a first
Rate Lawyer. Boarding with him that
could doo Business up Right.
Of which I sent You a Copy
I do not think he made more than
four times in gitting his Lawyer to
Draw up the Papers
I have Possession of the Place & Stock
with the Exception of 5 Oxen an 1 Waggon

which is on Green River in the care of
James Baker for which I have an Order
I have not as yet finishe the envoice
of All the property hear but think that
it will amount to^{near} five thousen Dollars.
Enclose I will send you
a memorandum of all the things on the
Place.   I Shall Commence gitting
Hay to Morrow this will be rather
a slow business as I have But one Syth
an Swath to commence with an the
Grass is Short
I have not as yet made anny
arrangements about$_x$ the ^{keeping} x Maile Animals.
the agent is to be up the nexttrip
I have notified them that the animals
could not stay on the Ranch unless I
had the charge of them an pay for the same

Brother Butler & my self have agreed that
the Expences of the house an the BlackSmithy
& Etc Should you on the Same as when
Bridger & Vasqus owned the establishment.
That is for the preasent

I wish You to wright to me as soon as
Possible what You want me to doo
an how You want me to dooit.
Wheather it will be best to Sell anny
of the Flour on the Place or not an if
not what would You do with a person
who had nothing to Eat
Their is Cattle hear that ar first rate
Beef which is probibly worth as much now
as they ever will be an will likely Sell well
to the trains that are coming for Beef.

You will see by refference to the envoice
that we have a good Supply of a few things
But we have no assortment.
Their Should be a good Stock of at
Least Indian Goods kept hear.
And the Emigrants Say Some of the
bejoyful

All is Well hear an it appears
like their was quite a calm
Bridger Left on the 4th Past

Livingstons traine of Goods will be hear
to knight
I do not think of any thing more at
the present time. But my Love to
all the Saints whare ever they may be
My Peace & Prosperity attend Us for Ever

The Boys at F. T. Supply ar all well
an their crops are quite prommicing.
They feel glad that F.T. Bridger
is Cagmet [sp?]
Your Brother as ever
D. H. Wells Lewis Robison

This document is Robison's inventory of merchandise at fort purchase, 1855.

Transcription from document on page 177

3600 lbs Flour 10 Dollars per hundred	$360.00
1½ Doz Bottles Stricknine	18.00
1 Pair Cairman [?] Small Scales	5.00
1 Do medicine Do	3.00
1 Do Stilgards [?]	2.00
45 lbs Wire 20 per lbs	9.00
3 Frying Pans	3.00
40 yds Fuse Rope 10 cts	4.00
7t lbs. Beever	75.00
4 Do Caster 3.00 per pound	12.00
2 Bair Skins	10.00
1 pair Trade Bullets moles	2.00
1½ Coz. Lead Pencils	1.50
¼ pound Calomet	1.00
3 Gallons Tar	3.00
20 Steel Traps out of repair	20.00
1 Spring Seet for Carriage	5.00
125 yds Gould & Silver Lace 50	62.50
8 read Plumes	4.00
6 Antilope Skins	6.00
10 Buck Skins	15.00
3 Pair Mocacins 75	2.25
2 Do Gloves 50	1.00
6 Buck Skin Hunting Shirts 3	18.00
1 Pair Pants	3.00
2500 Caps	2.50
1 Rifle	25.00
8 Doz Pack Playing Cards	5.00
½ Pound Flax Thread	1.00
125 yds Ribben 10	12.50
1 Pair Cotten Stocking	.25
10 lbs Alspice	2.00

$694.50 *

* Corrected figure is $693.50

5 lbs Candles	1.25
100 Do Tobacco	25.00
— 8 — Blue —	
17 American Blankets 3 Dol	51.00
3 Coats 2 Do	6.00
4 Doz Small Tin Panns 25 cts	11.00
7 Leather Sirsingles 1.00	7.00
17 Pair Martingales 1.00	17.00
8 Powder Horns 25	2.00
1 Tin Lantern	1.00
1 Sand Kiddle	2.00
6 Doz Papers Smoking Tobaccoe 6¼	4.50
25 lbs Assorted Beeds 1.00	25.00
2 Gross Brass Rings 1.00	2.00

4 Doz Thimbles			1.00
1 Can Lobsters			1.00
½ pound Brass Tacks			.50
½ Doz Tumblers			1.50
10 Butcher Knives			5.00
10 Gross Alls	1.00		10.00
3 Doz Papers needles			1.00
4 Doz Small Bells			1.00
6 Do Small Looking Glasses	5cts		3.60
20 lbs Vermillien	150		30.00
5 Do Powder	50		2.50
3 Doz clay Pipes			1.00
2 Do Small Metal Case Loking Glasses			1.00
9 Brass Hat Plates	2		2.25
12 cakes Shaving Soap			.50
12 Cotten Shalls	1.00		12.00
6 Do	50		3.00
22 Cotten Hdkf [?]	10		2.20
1 Silk Carral [?]			1.00
2 pair flannel trousers	150		3.00
			————
			$ 237.80

20 yds Scarlet	$2.00		40.00
100 Do Blue	2.00		200.00
2 Good Waggons	50.00		100.00
4 Old Do	15.00		60.00
12 Do Exeltrees	1.00		12.00
25 Loging chaines	1.00		25.00
2 Doz Trace chaines		25cts	6.00
1 Old whip Saw			2.00
Carpenters & Black Smiths Tools			35.00
1 Ton Old Iron			40.00
5 Pack Saddles			5.00
Dary & Kitchen Fixtures			60.00
			————
			585.00
Amount carge over from 1 Page			694.50*
Do Do 2 Do			237.80
			————
			$1517.30**
One hundred head of Cattle	$30.00		3000.00
Seven head of Horses	30		210.00
			————
			4727.30***

* Corrected figure is 693.50

** Corrected figure is $1516.30

*** Corrected figure is 4726.30

Commanding Officers, Fort Bridger, Wyoming

RANK	NAME	REGT.	FROM	TO
Major	William Hoffman, Bt. Lt. Col.	6th Inf.	June 10, 1858	Aug. 16, 1858
Major	Edward R. S. Canby, Bvt. Major	10th Inf.	Aug. 17, 1858	Mar. 6, 1860
Captain	R. C. Gatlin, Bvt. Major	7th Inf.	Mar. 7, 1860	June 3, 1860
Captain	Alfred Cumming	10th Inf.	June 4, 1860	Aug. 8, 1860
Captain	Franklin Gardner	10th Inf.	Aug. 9, 1860	Sept. 26, 1860
2nd Lieut.	Frank S. Armistead	10th Inf.	Sept. 27, 1860	Oct. 14, 1860
Captain	Franklin Gardner	10th Inf.	Oct. 14, 1860	April 7, 1861
2nd Lieut.	Frank S. Armistead	10th Inf.	April 7, 1861	May 28, 1861
Captain	Jesse A. Gove	10th Inf.	May 29, 1861	Aug. 9, 1861
1st Lieut.	Joseph C. Clark	4th Artillery	Aug. 9, 1861	Jan., 1861
Ord. Sgt.	John Boger	Ord. Dept.	Jan., 1862	
1st Lieut.	W. Kittredge	3rd Colo. Inf.	Jan. 13, 1863	Feb. 14, 1863
Captain	M. G. Lewis	3rd Colo. Inf.	Feb. 14, 1863	June 9, 1863
2nd Lieut.	Frederick Weed	2nd Colo. Cav.	June 9, 1863	June 19, 1863
2nd Lieut.	A. J. Austin	3rd Colo. Inf.	June 19, 1863	
Captain	George F. Price	2nd Colo. Cav.	June 19, 1863	Sept. 24, 1863
1st Lieut.	Willard Kittredge	3rd Colo. Inf.	Sept. 24, 1863	Oct. 4, 1863
Major	P. A. Gallagher	3rd Colo. Inf.	Oct. 4, 1863	Jan. 2, 1864
1st Lieut.	Willard Kittredge	3rd Colo. Inf.	Jan. 2, 1864	Feb. 10, 1864
Major	P. A. Gallagher	3rd Colo. Inf.	Feb. 10, 1864	July 26, 1864
Lieut.-Col.	A. A. C. Williams	1st Nev. Cav.	July 26, 1864	Oct. 10, 1864
Captain	E. B. Zabriskie	1st Nev. Cav.	Oct. 10, 1864	
Major	J. M. Oneil	2nd Colo. Cav.	Oct. 10, 1864	Feb. 10, 1865
Captain	Albert Brown	2nd Colo. Cav.	Feb. 10, 1865	Mar. 21, 1865
Major	Noyes Baldwin	1st Nev. Cav.	Mar. 21, 1865	May 20, 1865
1st Lieut.	James H. Stewart	1st Nev. Cav.	May 20, 1865	
Major	Noyes Baldwin	1st Nev. Cav.	May 21, 1865	Aug. 10, 1865
2nd Lieut.	James S. Warren	1st Nev. Cav.	Aug. 27, 1865	Aug. 30, 1865
Major	Noyes Baldwin	1st Nev. Cav.	Aug. 31, 1865	Nov. 12, 1865
Col. & Bvt. Brig. Gen.	P. Stagg	1st Mich. Vet. Cav.	Nov. 12, 1865	Dec. 30, 1865
Lt. Col.	W. Willard Smith	6th U. S. Vols.	Dec. 31, 1865	May 1, 1866
Capt. & Bvt. Maj.	Andrew S. Burt	18th U. S. Inf.	July, 1866	
Captain	Andrew S. Burt, Bvt. Maj.	18th U. S. Inf.	Sept., 1866	Nov., 1866
Captain	Anson Mills, Bvt. Lt. Col.	18th U. S. Inf.	Nov., 1866	Aug., 1867
Captain	Andrew S. Burt, Bvt. Maj.	18th U. S. Inf.	Aug., 1867	Aug. 17, 1867
Captain	Henry R. Mizner, Bvt. Lt. Col.	36th U. S. Inf.	Aug. 18, 1867	Nov. 9, 1867
Lieut.-Col.	Henry A. Morrow, Bvt. Col.	36th U. S. Inf.	Nov. 9, 1867	April 17, 1869
Captain	James P. W. Neile	36th U. S. Inf.	April 18, 1869	May 28, 1869
Lieut.-Col.	C. C. Gilbert, Bvt. Brig. Gen.	7th U. S. Inf.	May 28, 1869	Sept. 29, 1869
Captain	David S. Gordon, Bvt. Maj.	2nd U. S. Cav.	Sept. 30, 1869	Dec., 1869
Lieut.-Col.	Gilbert, Resumed command	7th U. S. nf.	Dec., 1869	Mar. 6, 1870
Captain	Gordon		Mar. 7, 1870	April 24, 1870
Major	R. S. LatMotte	13th U. S. Inf.	April 25, 1870	Sept. 1, 1872
Captain	E. W. Clift	13th U. S. Inf.	Sept. 1, 1872	Oct. 4, 1872
Lieut.-Col.	A. G. Brackett	2nd U. S. Cav.	Oct. 5, 1872	May 14, 1873
Colonel	Franklin F. Flint	4th U. S. Inf.	May 15, 1873	April 23, 1878
1st Lieut.	John Scott	4th U. S. Inf.	April 24, 1878	July, 1878
Captain	William H. Bisbee	4th U. S. Inf.	June 28, 1880	Nov. 20, 1882
Lieut.-Col.	Henry L. Chipman	7th U. S. Inf.	Nov. 21, 1882	April 13, 1883
Captain	Samuel Munson	9th U. S. Inf.	April, 1883	June 12, 1883
Lieut.-Col.	Thomas M. Anderson	9th U. S. Inf.	June 13, 1883	Aug. 31, 1884
Lieut.-Col.	Alexander Chambers	21st U. S. Inf.	Aug. 31, 1884	April 13, 1885
Captain	William W. Rogers	9th U. S. Inf.	April 25, 1885	May 3, 1885
Captain	Alfred Morton	9th U. S. Inf.	May 4, 1885	Oct. 12, 1885
Major	Edward P. Pearson	21st U. S. Inf.	Oct. 13, 1885	April, 1886
Captain	Alfred Morton	9th U. S. Inf.	April 13, 1886	July, 1886
Captain	Thomas H. Bradley	21st U. S. Inf.	July 18, 1886	Aug. 3, 1886
Captain	Henry S. Howe	17th U. S. Inf.	Aug. 3, 1886	Oct., 1886
Lieut.-Col.	John S. Poland	21st U. S. Inf.	Oct. 19, 1886	May, 1887
Major	John N. Andrews	21st U. S. Inf.	May 4, 1887	Oct. 1, 1890
1st Lieut.	Chas, St. J. Chubb	17th U. S. Inf.	Oct. 1, 1890	Nov. 6, 1890

From *Fort Bridger, Wyoming: A Brief History* by Robert S. Ellison

Fort Bridger Indian Agency, Fort Bridger, Utah Territory[1]

Indian Agent	Date
Luther Mann, Jr.	1861–1869
J. H. Patterson	1869
G. W. Fleming	1869–1870
J. W. Wham	1870

Shoshone-Bannock[2] **Agency, Wind River Reservation, Wyoming Territory**[3]

James Irwin	1871–1877
James I. Patten	1877–1879
Charles Hatton	1880–1882
James Irwin	1882–1884
S. R. Martin	1884–1885
Thomas M. Jones	1885–1889
John Fosher	1890–1893

1. After 25 July 1868, Wyoming Territory
2. After 1882, Shoshone Agency.
3. After 10 July 1890, State of Wyoming

Dr. Fred R. Gowans, an assistant professor of Indian education at Brigham Young University, has been teaching in the western United States since 1960. Since receiving his Ph.D. from Brigham Young University in 1972 Dr. Gowans has specialized in Western American history and current Indian affairs. He has presented numerous papers to Western historical groups and published several articles and book reviews in the *Utah Historical Quarterly* and *Annals of Wyoming.* In addition to his work on Fort Bridger, he is coauthor of a work in process on Fort Supply, and is currently completing a study of the fur trade rendezvous.

Dr. Eugene E. Campbell, a professor of history at Brigham Young University, received his Ph.D. from the University of Southern California in 1952. While serving as chairman of the history department from 1960 to 1967, he co-authored *The United States: An Interpretative History,* a college text published by Harper and Row, 1964. Dr. Campbell has published numerous articles on Mormon and Western history in learned journals. His article "Brigham Young's Outer Cordon: A Reappraisal" won the Dale Morgan Award for the best scholarly article published in the *Utah Historical Quarterly* in 1973 and also received the Mormon History Association Annual Award for the best article on a Mormon history subject published in 1973. Dr. Campbell has been listed in *Who's Who in America* since 1962.

Index

DUE